ALL

FALL

DOWN

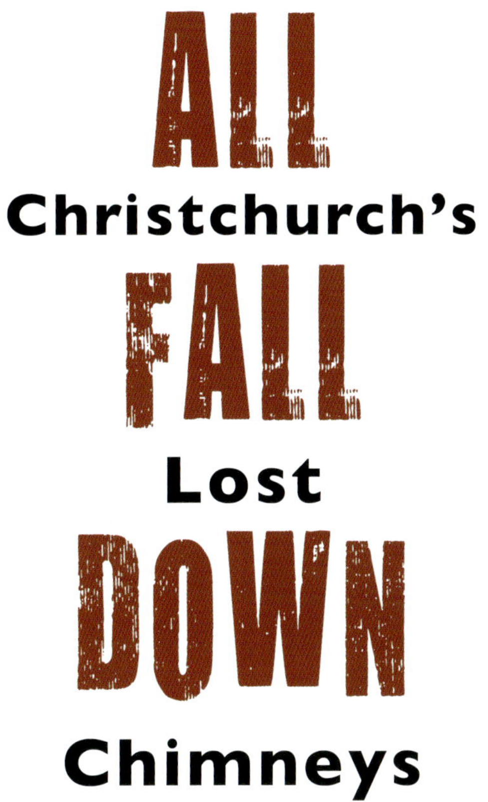

ALL FALL DOWN

Christchurch's Lost Chimneys

GEOFF RICE

CANTERBURY UNIVERSITY PRESS

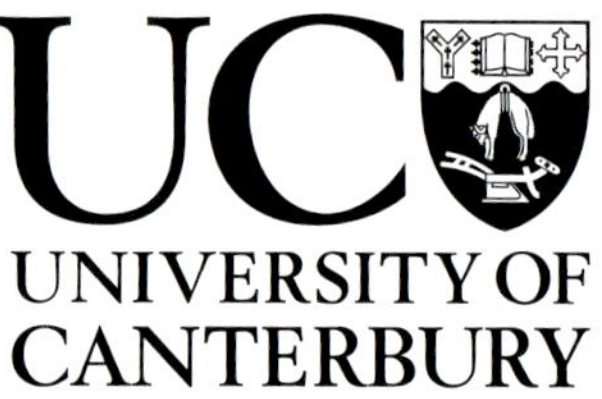

First published in 2011 by
CANTERBURY UNIVERSITY PRESS
University of Canterbury
Private Bag 4800, Christchurch
NEW ZEALAND
www.cup.canterbury.ac.nz

ISBN 978-1-927145-10-4

A catalogue record for this book is available from the
National Library of New Zealand.

Design and layout by Quentin Wilson, Christchurch
Printed by Everbest, China

CONTENTS

PREFACE

This book has been compiled for the many Christchurch and Canterbury residents who lost a chimney in the earthquakes and aftershocks of 2010 and 2011, and for everyone else, as a reminder of what the city has lost and a celebration of what has survived. It may seem an odd subject, and this certainly isn't the first chimney book to be published, but as far as I know it is the first about chimneys in New Zealand. We tend to take chimneys for granted, and don't even think about them until they need sweeping or painting, or come crashing through the ceiling. Chimneys have always been a familiar part of Christchurch, but now many of them have gone and the city's streets look somehow different, lacking the vertical accents that once enlivened our flat and mostly single-storey suburbs.

Having taken photos of interesting chimneys and their pots over many years, and read most of the few books in English devoted to the humble chimney, I was prompted by the 2010 earthquakes and the loss of our own chimney to dig out old notes and start assembling what I hoped would be an informative history of the European (in fact, mostly British) chimney, and a survey of Christchurch chimneys, both domestic and industrial, since 1850, to provide a context for understanding where our chimneys came from and how our chimneys formed part of a broader heritage.

But events overtook this modest contribution to Christchurch's heritage history. The book had been accepted for publication, passed the editing stage and was just about to be sent to the designer when Christchurch's central business district was devastated by the 22 February 2011 earthquake, with serious loss of life. This was a much more catastrophic event than that of September 2010, with lateral shaking measured in Heathcote Valley at 2.2 times the force of gravity. The September epicentre had been under the Canterbury Plains, near Greendale, and the 7.1 magnitude quake had damaged many brick buildings in Christchurch, but nobody had died and for many people life returned to normal reasonably quickly. By contrast, the February 2011 epicentre was underneath Lyttelton, and though its magnitude was less, at 6.3, this much shallower quake did far more damage to the city and to the port. Two modern office buildings collapsed, killing over 180 people, including many visitors to the city and Asian students at a language school. Others were killed when buildings collapsed onto their vehicles.

Christchurch's earthquake became headline news around the world and specialised urban rescue teams flew in from many different countries to assist in the search for survivors among the rubble of the central city. Christchurch's Neo-Gothic Anglican cathedral, the city's centrepiece and symbol, had lost its spire and tower. The Roman Catholic basilica in Barbadoes Street, widely regarded as the finest Neo-Classical building in New Zealand, had lost both its towers and had its dome twisted. Churches that had been badly damaged in September 2010, most notably Holy Trinity at Avonside and the Oxford Terrace Baptist Church, had simply collapsed. Three pipe-organ experts were killed when the Durham Street Methodist Church, the first stone structure on the Canterbury Plains, fell on top of them. It, too, had been seriously compromised in the September quake. Many older commercial buildings in the central city had either partially or completely collapsed, leaving some streets looking like photos of London or Coventry after the bombing raids of the 1940s. Some of the city's tall modern structures had also been damaged. The Hotel Grand Chancellor, slumped at one end, posed a threat to rescue workers in nearby blocks.

  ALL FALL DOWN Christchurch's Lost Chimneys

In the desperate race to rescue those trapped inside fallen buildings, the government declared a state of national emergency, the first in New Zealand's history, enabling the immediate demolition of buildings that presented a risk to rescue teams. Unfortunately this policy led to the hasty demolition of a number of heritage buildings that were not a threat to anyone, including the Addington flour mill and the 1878 Sydenham Heritage Church, thereby rubbing salt in the wounds of a city stunned by its human and heritage losses.

For most people in the devastated eastern suburbs, the weeks following 22 February 2011 were a time of great hardship and day-to-day improvisation, as they struggled without water, power, phones or sewerage. Help flooded in from all sides, however, as students and farmers laboured to shovel away the hundreds of tonnes of fine grey silt that had been forced to the surface by liquefaction in many streets and gardens. Skilled technicians worked night and day to restore power to a stricken city, while council staff toiled in contaminated mud to repair broken water and sewage pipes. Clean water was the most urgent requirement, and truckloads of bottled water were brought to the city, along with ample supplies of petrol and diesel. Gradually the most basic needs of eastern residents were met, with the distribution of portaloos and chemical toilets.

Overseas news teams were astonished by the swift response of civil defence and local welfare agencies: the leader of the British urban rescue team was heard to say that this was 'the best-organised emergency' he'd ever attended. This was

mainly because New Zealand has excellent civil defence plans for disasters and pandemics, and also because Christchurch had had a dress rehearsal for an earthquake disaster barely six months earlier. The mayor and his emergency team had only a short walk from the new civic offices to set up their disaster headquarters once again at the Christchurch Art Gallery/ Te Puna o Waiwhetu. A well-oiled machine had swung into action with remarkable rapidity. Then, just as the city was attempting to restore some semblance of normal life, with Canterbury University reopening and businesses relocating into the suburbs, there came the horrifying footage of Japan's earthquake and tsunami disaster on 11 March, followed by weeks of anxiety about its damaged nuclear power station at Fukushima. Christchurch's national memorial service for the February earthquake, held in Hagley Park on 18 March and attended by Prince William, provided an opportunity to remember the thousands of dead and missing in Japan as well as the Christchurch victims of 22 February.

A little book about old chimneys was never likely to rate highly on anybody's list of priorities after this disaster, especially when its editor and designer

were both homeless and the publisher could not get into her office. In view of the loss of life, it seemed right and proper to delay the project for a few months, until some normality had returned and people had had time to reflect on and come to terms with the tragic events of 2011. This delay enabled me to recast the text, and to change the order of some of the photographs. Many of the chimneys that had been photographed as survivors of the September 2010 earthquake were now in ruins or had been removed completely. Yet as time went by it seemed to me that this little book was now all the more worthwhile, as a record and

reminder of what the city had lost, not just from the earthquakes but from the previous ravages of time and property developers.

It has long been a passing joke among New Zealand historians that Canterbury's founding fathers chose to locate their future city in the middle of a swamp. Little did they or anyone else suspect that they also located it on a fault-line, in fact, several fault-lines. Once regarded as a city of low earthquake risk, Christchurch has now become New Zealand's earthquake capital, with over 8000 recorded tremors since September 2010. The damage to buildings, homes, schools and businesses has been amazingly random, with some apparently unharmed structures standing next to severely damaged or collapsed ones. Likewise with the city's chimneys. Some suburbs were hit harder than others, depending on the subsoils and the direction of the shockwaves. In a few older streets every chimney fell, often in the same direction, while in newer suburbs modern reinforced chimneys survived the main quakes and aftershocks apparently unscathed.

It was only as I assembled the illustrations for this book that I realised how much of Christchurch's industrial chimney heritage had also been lost, long before the earthquakes of 2010 and 2011. We would not wish to go back to coal-fired boilers when electricity provides environmentally clean power for industry, but the city once had a large number of tall brick chimneys that were graceful masterpieces of the bricklayers' art, and now they have all gone. Chapter Three attempts to remind us of this lost industrial heritage.

I would like to acknowledge the generosity of the *Christchurch Star* in making images from its historic collection freely available for this book.

My thanks to Dave Wethey for the cover photo.

Warm thanks are also due to the talented production team at Canterbury University Press: editor Anna Rogers, designer Quentin Wilson, intern Frith Hughes, and publisher Rachel Scott. They patiently tolerated my numerous changes and last-minute additions. At one point Rachel implored me to lock my camera away in a cupboard so they could actually send the book to the printer, as I kept on discovering interesting survivors. I must also thank my good friend Gordon Ogilvie for supplying the Glenmore Quake-Proof Chimneys advertisement, and for showing me the locations of the seven or more brickworks that used to exist at the foot of the Port Hills.

Unless otherwise acknowledged, the line drawings and most of the colour photographs are my own. A few of the colour photographs and the historic illustrations in Chapter One, found in Wikipedia Commons, are in the public domain. The historic photos in Chapters Two and Three have been sourced from the Canterbury Museum, Christchurch City Libraries, the *Christchurch Star* and the Alexander Turnbull Library, Wellington. The photograph on p.116 is reproduced with the permission of the Superior Clay Corporation, Ohio.

DEDICATION

Originally I wanted to dedicate this book to my elder brother, Bob Rice, because he had a brief but glorious spell as a chimney sweep in the 1960s. He called his one-man outfit City Chimney Cleaners, and dressed all in black, in accordance with tradition. He worked hard to gain a reputation for a clean and thorough job. Our mother spent hours on the telephone drumming up customers and I remember doing the signwriting on his ladders. He did so well that within a year he was bought out by someone who made him an offer too good to refuse, and he happily returned to his first love, long-distance truck driving. After a career as a foreman road-marker, he has retired to Australia's Sunshine Coast, where his neighbours assure him, even when it is pouring with rain, 'It's not cold!'

I'm sure he won't mind, but there is someone more deserving of this dedication, a man who lost his life in the February 2011 earthquake. Ross Bush, master bricklayer and chimney-builder, had done the brickwork for our kitchen extension in 2004 and we had many interesting yarns while I scraped bricks and he laid them in neat straight lines. He was a very fit man, a veteran long-distance cyclist, and was highly-regarded in both

trade and sporting circles. On 22 February Ross was in the wrong place at the wrong time, parking his car in Riccarton Road when the earthquake struck. A brick building collapsed on top of him. As his grieving family noted, he had made his living from bricks, and they had caused his death. He was a good man and is sorely missed.

I would therefore like to dedicate this book to the memory of Ross Bush, and to his predecessors, the generations of skilled bricklayers who helped to form the fabric of our city.

The Linwood cleaning sheds in the late 1960s.

PROLOGUE

I grew up in the smoky grimy Christchurch of the 1950s. We lived in Waltham, a working-class suburb close to the railway yards. Whenever the north-easterly was blowing, which was just about every day the sun was shining, we received abundant smoke and smuts from the Linwood cleaning sheds, where the steam locomotives emptied their ashes at the end of each working day and reloaded their tenders with coal and water. I can remember seeing my mother reduced to tears when she saw her freshly laundered white sheets covered in smuts. She had to pull them off the line to start the wash all over again.

On some winter nights in Waltham the smog was so thick that we could barely see the houses on the opposite side of the street. No wonder we were all asthmatics. Everyone around us burned coal in open grates to heat their houses. In my mind's eye I can still see those red smoky sunsets at the western end of Walpole Street, with power poles and wires and chimneys silhouetted. Smoke would be rising from almost every chimney, to join the growing black blanket of the night.

In my childhood industrial chimneys were all around me. At the top end of Waltham Road, beside the new railway overbridge, there was the gasworks, with numerous chimneys, pipes and vents. At the bottom end of Waltham Road, near the Heathcote River, stood the maltworks. Over the railway crossing in Wilsons Road near the Linwood Station there was a pickle factory. In Sydenham there were several small factories with coal-fired steam boilers. Madras Street was home to William H. Jackson's foundry (*below*). All puffed out their individual contributions to the smells and smogs of 1950s Christchurch.

Further afield, down in Woolston, already by then the city's heavy industrial suburb, there were the tanneries and the rubber factory, the Davis

Gelatine works, which discharged noisome effluent and foam into the Heathcote River, and Anderson's foundry, all with industrial chimneys of various shapes and heights.

These familiar sights of my childhood have all disappeared, swept away by changing technologies and clean air legislation. Christchurch is now a much healthier place in which to live, but to me it looks very different. All those squat brick factory chimneys have gone from Sydenham, replaced in a few cases by tall metal tubes. Most factories these days are entirely electric. The steam trains have been replaced by diesels. Never again will we hear the New Year greeted by the massed whistles of steam locomotives and factories. Never again will I see billows of steam from the gasworks, seen here in 1973, as each new batch of heated coal was drenched with water to produce town gas, coke and all sorts of interesting by-products. In the photo

below the building being demolished at left was the old generator plant for Christchurch's electric trams.

As a small boy I used to stand and marvel at these man-made clouds, white and wind-blown, when the Canterbury summer sky was pure blue. My classmates thought I was peculiar when I said I loved the smell of tar from the gasworks and the coal smoke from the railways, so it will come as no surprise to them that I have written a book about chimneys. How many of you can remember seeing the musical film *Mary Poppins*, starring Julie Andrews and Dick van Dyke? It was released in 1964, my last year at high school. One of the liveliest sequences is the rooftop dance of the London chimney sweeps, around the chimney stacks of a studio set. So many chimneys! I was fascinated by the sheer variety of English chimney pots. Most New Zealand pots are plain round drainpipes

stood on end, but these were minor masterpieces of the potter's art, gargoyles on the gable, curiosities in clay, or sooty statements.

On my first trip to London and Britain in the early 1970s I often took photographs of historic buildings, noticing their chimneys and the diversity of their pots, and wanted to know more

about their origins and regional patterns. But other more urgent priorities got in the way, for many years to come, and it was not until the 1990s that I made time in between other research in the British Library to read a pile of books (or should that be a stack?) about chimneys.

Of course I had always been aware of the interesting chimney pots on older Christchurch houses, and wondered if they had been imported from England or made locally. I especially liked those slightly rotund terracotta ones with a flower pattern stamped on their sides. It was not until many years later that I discovered that these were Homebush pots, made by the Homebush Brick, Tile, Terra-cotta and Pottery Works (*above right*) at Glentunnel in the 1880s and 1890s.

The Deans family started this business in the

1870s, along with their Bush Gully coal mine in the Malvern Hills. There were deposits of good pottery clay in the same hills. According to Gordon

Ogilvie's *Pioneers of the Plains* (1996), the pottery works' 1877 catalogue offered a wide variety of bricks, cornices, roof tiles, grease traps and 'ornate chimney pots'. Two of Christchurch's leading architects in the late nineteenth century, Samuel Hurst Seager and Robert W. England junior, helped to design some of the Homebush terracotta products, including their chimney pots. Most New Zealand chimney pots are copies of British originals, but the Homebush pot is an indigenous product. The flower pattern is a simplified version of the Japanese imperial chrysanthemum, and may also be seen on the Deans memorial gates of the former A & P Showgrounds in Lincoln Road. But the company later deleted all the chimney pots and domestic ware to concentrate on bricks and field-drainage pipes. The pottery was sold to McSkimming Industries in

1924 and production ceased in 1983. The site was cleared and nothing remains of this once-flourishing mid-Canterbury industry.

It is sad to think that the elegant Deans homestead at Homebush, which had at least seven Homebush chimney pots, was one of the most spectacular victims of the 2010 earthquake. Many Christchurch houses built in the 1890s and early 1900s, especially the larger ones, had Homebush pots, and most of these were lost in September 2010, making them even rarer as heritage objects. A few years ago I was fortunate enough to buy one from the modernisation of a house in Harewood Road, and it now sits in our back garden, as a decorative feature and a reminder of Christchurch's chimney pot heritage.

But where did all the other Christchurch chimney pots come from? The very earliest may have been imported from England, along with the migrants of New Zealand's settler society, or from Australia, where potteries were replicating English designs from the early nineteenth century.

From the 1870s New Zealand potteries

Homebush Brick, Tile, Terra-cotta and Pottery Works in the 1890s.

began to produce chimney pots, along with bricks
and drainage pipes, but usually imitating familiar
English styles. Local potteries seem to have been
more interested in producing bricks and tiles than
chimney pots, though Luke Adams in Sydenham
became famous for his demijohns and domestic
ware.

Christchurch bricklayers obviously took great
pride in constructing sturdy but distinctive chimneys in the late nineteenth century, especially for
the grand houses of wealthier citizens. In Chapter
Two we shall see some examples of their crafts-
manship.

But where did chimneys originate? How do
they work? What is the difference between a good
'drawing' chimney and a bad smoky chimney?
What was the function of the chimney pot? It is
time to sit back and enjoy a brief history of the
European chimney.

Hedingham Castle in Essex.

CHAPTER ONE

A Brief History of the European Chimney

Smoke rises. How's that for a statement of the obvious? In normal atmospheric conditions hot gases expand and tend to rise. Smoke from burning wood or coal may be fragrant in small doses to some nostrils, but for most humans it irritates the throat and lungs, making us cough, so it is better avoided. A bonfire in the open is merely a temporary nuisance – unless it sets fire to a shed, or a forest – and the smoke can be avoided by stepping around to the upwind side, but a constant fire in a confined space creates a smoke problem for the humans who are trying to keep warm beside it or cook a meal on it. The chimney was humanity's simple solution to this localised environmental pollution. Let the smoke escape the room, rise into the outside air and become somebody else's problem.

Very little is known about chimneys in the ancient world since next to no examples have survived. Indeed, there is a school of thought that the modern chimney as we know it was not invented until the Renaissance of the fifteenth century, but this, as we shall see, is a myth. The earliest reference to a chimney in the Bible is found in Hosea 13.3: 'Therefore they shall be as the morning cloud, and as the early dew that passeth away, as the chaff that is driven with the whirlwind out of the floor, and as the smoke out of the chimney.' (But the Hebrew is ambiguous, and one modern translation has window instead of chimney.) The Greek word for an oven or fireplace was *kaminos*, borrowed by the Romans to become *caminus* in Latin. This could refer to the whole heating apparatus, fireplace and chimney combined.

The Romans had elaborate heating systems for their baths, including the hypocaust or underfloor heating. Both Pliny and Valerius Maximus attribute the invention of the latter to Sergius Orata (d. 95 BC), an oyster-breeder and property developer, who is reputed to have bought old villas, installed underfloor heating and sold them at a profit. But there are no recognisable chimney stalks among Roman ruins or archaeological sites. Even at Pompeii there are only fireplaces: nearly everything above roof level was destroyed in the eruption of Vesuvius in AD 79. Above the fireplaces are vents inside the walls, which presumably had some sort of chimney at the top, to carry the smoke away over the rooftops.

Among the archaeological remains excavated at Pompeii there is a lucky survivor, a rare terracotta chimney pot of the type that the French later called a *louvre* (*below*). This presumably sat on top of the chimney, to prevent rain from dousing the fire. The cross-draught through its holes would have helped to draw the smoke up from the hearth.

This rare survivor (*above*) is a shallow fireplace from the Roman fort that was later rebuilt as Colchester Castle in Essex, England. The narrow round-section flue survives in the wall.

The idea that the chimney was invented in the Renaissance is flatly contradicted by the large number of surviving medieval chimneys, especially in England. Most dwellings in the post-Roman era were of timber and thatch with a hearth in the middle of the floor. There was usually a hole in the roof directly above the fire, or the smoke had to find its own way out through the thatch. Stone buildings were expensive, and the preserve of the church and nobility. Building activity seems to have ceased in Western Europe during the Viking era, but as trade revived and the population began to grow again in the eleventh century timber structures, including castles, were gradually reconstructed in stone.

The earliest surviving examples of medieval chimneys are those built into castles. Hedingham Castle in Essex (c.1130) has flues built into the walls for fireplaces at two levels in the south buttress. The smoke escaped from holes near the top of the wall.

Christchurch Castle in Hampshire (*above*) has the earliest surviving example of a round Norman chimney, from c.1160.

 ALL FALL DOWN CHRISTCHURCH'S LOST CHIMNEYS

Another early round chimney is the Lanterne des Morts in Bayeux, Normandy (*above*). Local legend has it that whenever a resident of the town died, a light would be seen in the vents of this chimney. The chimney at Christchurch Castle may originally have had a conical cap, like the one at Bayeux.

During the twelfth and thirteenth centuries Europe experienced a booming economy and rapid population increase that saw the growth of towns into cities, the expansion of trade, the Crusades, the invention of universities and the construction of soaring Gothic cathedrals. Standards of living for the social elite improved, and these included being kept warm in the winter.

Most of the population, however, were peasants on the land, still living in thatched cottages with a hearth in the floor. These must have had very murky interiors, and the residents probably looked as smoked as the bacon they hung from the rafters. Poor people were used to being cold most of the time, and this included the monks in their stone monasteries. Too much comfort was equated with softness and sin. The infirmary and the abbot's rooms, however, would have been warmed by fireplaces in the winter. In monasteries, as in most houses, the kitchen was probably the warmest place all year round.

The earliest-surviving English example of a domestic chimney-piece is the so-called Jew's House at Lincoln (*above*), which dates from c.1170. (The present brick chimney is a later addition.) The fireplace was above the front door, to heat the first floor hall, but the original chimney has long since disappeared. It may have been like the one at Bayeux, which dates from the same period.

The stone or terracotta louvres on top of chimneys were there mainly to keep out rain or snow, but they also helped to draw the smoke from the fireplace by creating a cross-draught. This rare example of a very elaborate medieval louvre (*below*) is held in the Colchester Museum.

Abingdon Abbey in Oxfordshire (*above*) has a chimney that looks more like a tower, with several flues and a window-like vent. Good examples of recognisably modern chimneys survive at Kingham (*left, above right*), also in Oxfordshire, and at Boothby Pagnell manor house in Lincolnshire (*above, far right*). Margaret Wood's standard account of *The English Medieval House* (1963) lists nearly 100 surviving examples of merchants' houses and first-floor halls, most of which have fireplaces but no surviving chimneys.

 ALL FALL DOWN CHRISTCHURCH'S LOST CHIMNEYS

This terracotta figure (*above*), similar to the gargoyles on medieval churches and cathedrals, used to sit on a chimney louvre in High Street, Oxford, and is now in the Ashmolean Museum. It was widely believed that witches perched on chimney tops at night, so these figures probably had exactly the same purpose as a gargoyle, to frighten them away.

Sometime in the twelfth century, however, someone discovered that a plain earthenware pipe which narrowed towards the top was much more effective in drawing the smoke up from the fireplace. This made use of the venturi effect whereby the compression of moving hot gases increases their velocity. (This is the basic principle of a jet engine.) Thus was born the modern chimney pot, as distinct from the louvre.

The illustrations of the *Très Riches Heures*, a richly decorated book of hours made by the Limbourg brothers for the Duc de Berry about 1410, contain two examples of chimneys from opposite ends of the social hierarchy. One cutaway view of a farmhouse (*below*) shows a peasant family warming themselves at the fire while snow falls outside. Their chimney is a wickerwork structure that must have been plastered with clay on the inside to prevent it from catching fire.

The second illustration (*above*) shows a large late-medieval castle with a forest of round stone chimneys.

Later medieval fireplaces could be massive affairs, with sloping stone hoods to catch the smoke, and even the small ones were often

decorated with coats of arms, as in this example (*opposite page, bottom*) from Old Beaupré Castle in South Wales.

In Italy a chimney was called a *camino* (from the Latin *caminus*) or *fumaiuolo*. To this day, an Italian chimney sweep is called a *spazzacamino*. Chimneys could be either round or square in section. The simple use of tiles to form a tent over the opening may be a direct descendant of Roman practice.

These adjacent buildings in Bologna (*above*)

feature three different chimney types: brick vents, round pipes and the terracotta tent.

These terracotta roofed chimneys (*below*) are

typical of Tuscany and northern Italy, where winter snowfalls can be heavy.

Venice developed a distinctive type of chimney with a cone-shaped top, rather like the funnel of early steam locomotives in the American West. The purpose behind the design was identical: to catch sparks. The risk of fire was always very great in medieval cities, where most of the buildings were made of wood. City authorities encouraged those who could afford it to build in brick or stone, and to use slate or tiles on the roof. This detail (*below*) from Vittorio Carpaccio's painting *Miracle of the Relic of the True Cross* (1494) shows a forest of these chimneys above the rooftops of Venice. Only a few of these have survived to the present day.

A selection of typical European chimney styles.

In fifteenth-century England bricks became plentiful and cheap, and ever since have been the preferred material for British chimneys at all social levels. Indeed, there seems to have been something of a craze for chimneys as status symbols in the sixteenth century, probably started by Cardinal Thomas Wolsey's extravagant pioneering example at Hampton Court Palace in the 1520s (*right*). Though many of

its chimneys are modern rebuilds, they faithfully replicate the original intricate designs, which remain masterpieces of the bricklayer's art.

Tudor brickmakers and bricklayers must have had fun trying to outdo each other with ever more elaborate and impressive chimneys. These superb examples of twisted chimneys are from the Abbey of St Osyth in Essex (*above and below*). Some observers have called these barley-corn chimneys from their resemblance to the twists of corn-dollies used in harvest festivals and as folk decorations.

How did the Tudors achieve this stunning effect? By careful design. Each brick had to be hand-moulded into the right curve before firing to get that sinuous effect. These were therefore very expensive chimneys, status symbols that proclaimed the wealth of the owner. This fine example (*above*) comes from Sudbury in Suffolk.

These chimneys (*above*) at Great Waltham in Essex are plain Tudor stalks, more for practicality than show. This is clearly not a country prone to earthquakes.

St James's Palace in London (*above*) was built by Henry VIII in the 1530s, but its chimneys were much plainer than those at Hampton Court. (The pots in this photo are modern.)

The structural strength of a chimney stack has often helped in the survival of middle-class chimneys, as in this example at Lavenham in Suffolk (*above*). In some cases old wooden houses were pulled down, except for the chimney stack. The new house was then built around it.

Chimneys were often the dominant architectural features of large Tudor houses, as seen here (*above*) at Mapledurham beside the River Thames near Reading.

Hylands House, Essex, (*above*) was built by the lawyer Sir John Comyns in 1730 as a red brick house, but a later owner commissioned the architect Humphrey Repton to cover it and its chimneys in white stucco in 1797.

English chimney pots developed distinctive regional variations, depending on the local clays and the inventiveness of regional potteries. While most were simple tapering tubes with a rim or lip, some had toothed or even crenellated tops (*left*).

This nineteenth-century photo of Strasbourg (*above*) shows the steep tiled roofs of the old city and a variety of chimneys, some open vents and some square louvres.

Late sixteenth-century views of London demonstrate that almost every building had a chimney, and on larger edifices they were often grouped together in stacks. Visitors often commented on London's thick smog in winter, as nearly all these fireplaces belched smoke from coal fires. Elizabeth I had banned coal fires while parliament was in session, as the country members found the smog intolerable. The coal came by ship from mines in the north-east of England: hence the expression 'sea coal'. By 1600 over 200 ships were employed in the coal trade.

English bricklayers had an almost mystical conviction that a bend in a chimney improved the air-flow, but any bend tends to accumulate soot

and bits of old mortar from between the bricks.
Keeping chimneys clean was a problem that must
have started with the very first stone flues in the
twelfth century. Chimney sweeping became a
recognised occupation in late-medieval London,
but we know most about it from the seventeenth
century onwards, when sweeps petitioned the city
authorities for a recognised scale of pay and better
working conditions.

Coal fires left thicker deposits of soot inside
the chimney flues, and required more frequent
sweeping, but London's chimney sweeps complained
that the work was difficult and poorly paid. In 1618
James I received *The Petition of the Poor Chimney
Sweepers of the City of London to the King* asking for
the appointment of an overseer who was to be paid
from the proceeds of the sale of soot as fertiliser.
(Soot contains ammonia salts and nitrogen.) The
petition was supported by prominent politician and
writer Sir Robert Naunton, but nothing came of it.

Prince Rupert, nephew of Charles I, devised
a fireplace with a raised grate and a cast-iron
baffle-plate to regulate the flow of hot gases up the
chimney. This, however, created the further problem of back-pressure, so he added another hinged
plate above the front of the firebox, which created a
forced draught to help get the fire going. Once the
fire was burning brightly, the plate could be hooked
back for normal operation.

Chimney sweeping was always a strange occupation. People like the Puritans, who believed that
cleanliness was next to godliness, regarded chimney sweeps with horror and revulsion, as if they
belonged to the Devil and the smoky dominions of

Seyley and his boy. Etching by Marcellus Lauron, 1687.

Hell. But it was a necessary occupation: somebody
had to do it. Having the chimneys swept must have
been a sore trial for the houseproud, since it was a
notoriously dirty business. The usual method was
to drop a rope down the chimney and attach, to
the top, a brush or a bundle of sticks, which was
then pulled vigorously down the flue, bringing
with it clouds of black soot. In those days before
vacuum cleaners it must have been advisable to
clear the room of carpets and furniture beforehand.
There are stories of geese being used instead of the
bundle of sticks: the blacker the goose on exit the
cleaner the chimney was thought to be. The sweep
collected the soot for resale to market gardeners.
Many myths surrounded the profession, such as the

one that a kiss from a chimney sweep gave good luck to the bride on her wedding day.

After the disruption of the Civil War and Interregnum more peaceful times returned with Charles II and the Restoration of 1660, but the chimney sweeps of London still had problems. In 1663 *The Chimney-Sweepers' Sad Complaint* protested at the demolition of the Eleanor Cross in Cheapside where they had always propped their brooms against the railings while they waited for business. The Great Fire of London in 1666 demonstrated on a grand scale the risks of having so many domestic fires in a densely crowded city built mostly of wood. Though it was decided that the rebuilding would follow the original medieval street plan, with all its narrow winding lanes, the buildings now had to be fireproof, in stone or brick, and with slate or tile roofs. Chimneys were sometimes the only things left standing after fire had destroyed a wooden house.

At the same time, across the Channel in France, Louis XIV was expanding his magnificent palace at Versailles (*below*) as a symbol of the wealth and power of the French monarchy, and also as a device to tame the nobility: he insisted that the leading families live with him in the palace, where he could keep an eye on them. Naturally they expected to be kept as warm as they would be at home in their own chateaux, so Versailles was built with rank upon rank of chimney stacks.

The design of fireplaces underwent a revolution in the eighteenth century, with elegant surrounds designed by leading architects such as the Adam brothers, but the brickwork behind them was usually left to the bricklayers. New scientific principles were slow to be adopted where craft traditions were strong.

Some of the best thinkers of the eighteenth century, including Benjamin Franklin, bent their minds to the problem of getting the most heat for their money and getting rid of the smoke most efficiently. Practical treatises on chimney-building began to appear. One of the most popular, published in 1771, was James Anderson's *A Practical Treatise on Chimneys, containing Full Directions for Preventing or Removing Smoke in Houses.* Anderson insisted on correct mathematical relationships between the width of the hearth, the angle of the smoke hood and the height of the chimney. He understood the dynamics of hot gases, noting that a gradually narrowing flue increased velocity, as did a tapering chimney pot.

Among Anderson's many imitators was Robert Clavering, who in 1779 published a 100-page treatise called *An Essay on the Construction and Building of Chimneys, including an Inquiry into the Common Causes of their Smoaking, and the Most Effectual Remedies for Removing so intolerable a Nuisance: with a Table to Proportion Chimneys to the Size of the Room.* Notwithstanding its remarkably long-winded title, this was a more practical work, with many useful illustrations. Clavering had taken advice from 'able workmen and ingenious bricklayers' to establish what was then best-practice

in chimney construction. Before these eighteenth-century publications there were few textbooks or manuals on bricklaying: the art was handed down from father to son, and most of them, in any case, may not have been able to read.

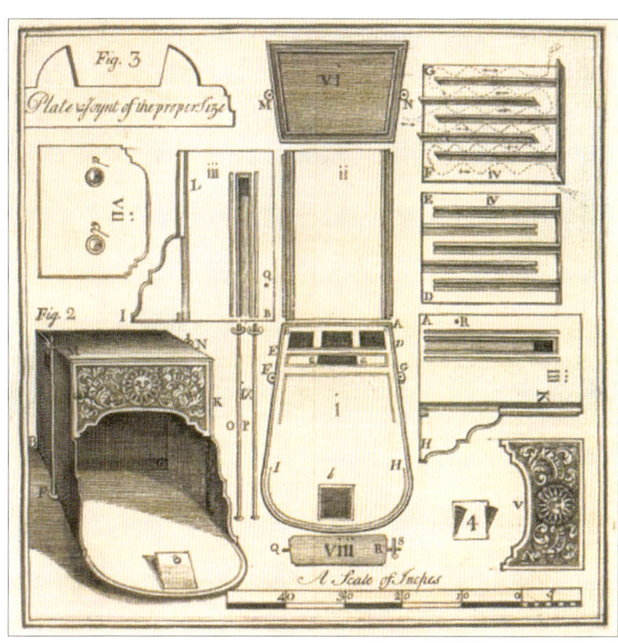

Observing that a lot of heat was wasted in an open fireplace, Benjamin Franklin designed the first space heater (*above*), the ancestor of our modern log-burners. His Pennsylvania fireplace was a simple but ingenious design using metal pipes to draw cold air from under the house, heating the pipes at the back of the firebox and then passing the heated air into the room. This eliminated draughts from doorways. The fire gases were directed down the back of a sealed baffle into the base of the fireplace and then up the flue. A sliding metal plate controlled the rate at which the hot gases went up the chimney. With characteristic generosity Franklin refused to patent his invention, making it freely available for anyone to copy. Modern versions of the Franklin stove are still made in Europe and North America. Interestingly, Colonial American chimney builders refused to adopt the typical English chimney pot, and visitors often comment on their absence on old American houses. (Perhaps they were making a political point?)

Another notable 'chimney-doctor' of the eighteenth century was Count Rumford, who claimed to have 'cured' over 500 defective and smoky chimneys in his time. He laid down strict rules for their construction, mostly borrowed from Clavering: the fireplace opening should be square, the depth should be half the width of the open-ing, the sides should be splayed outwards, the area inside the flue should be one-tenth the area, the upper two-thirds of the fire-back should slope outwards, and so forth.

The stately homes of the English gentry and aristocracy in the eighteenth century were designed to impress, and chimneys were a prominent feature of many grand houses, often becoming local land-marks, visible for miles around. A good example of this is Winslow Hall in Buckinghamshire, (*below*) built in 1700 for Secretary of the Treasury William Lowndes, with advice from Sir Christopher Wren.

Chimneys continued to proliferate in the eighteenth century, even becoming a part of the grandest Neo-classical architecture, as seen here in the Royal Crescent at Bath (1765) (*above*), designed by John Wood the younger.

London's Bedford Square (*above*) is one among many examples of eighteenth-century architecture featuring orderly rows of chimneys. Aristocratic households with so many fireplaces needed a small army of servants to keep the house warm in the winter, laying and lighting the fires in the morning, fetching coal during the day and cleaning the grates at night.

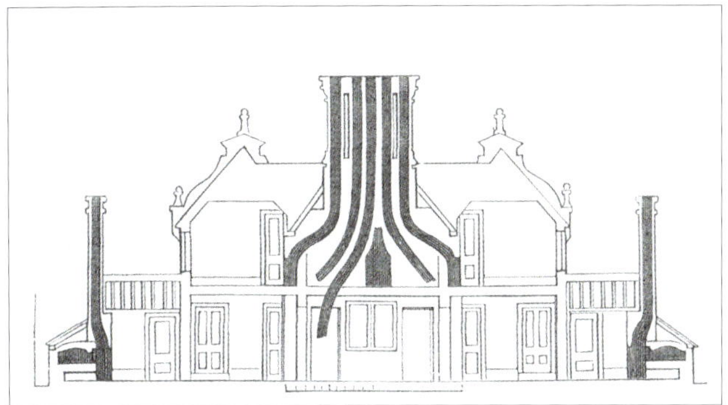

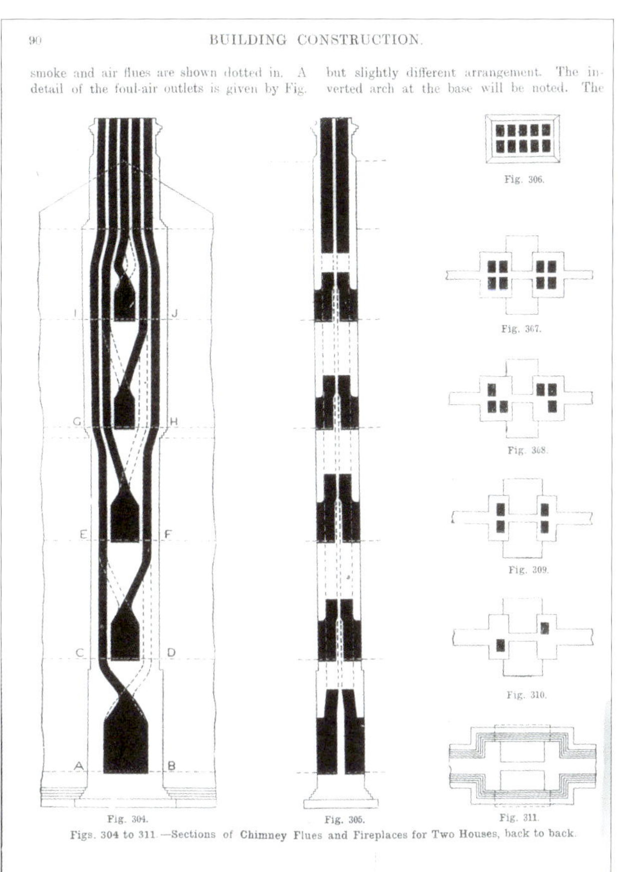

Multi-flued chimneys were complex construc-
tions, demanding the utmost in skill and exact
measurement from the bricklayers. These eleva-
tions (*above*) from C. J. Richardson's treatise on *The
Englishman's House* (1872) show how a single stack
could serve half a dozen fireplaces.

The nineteenth century produced a large
literature of textbooks and manuals on bricklaying and chimney design, establishing the practices
that are still followed today. Architects made
chimneys even more integral features of domestic houses, especially those that were part of the
Gothic Revival. These illustrations (*above right*)
from Henry Adams' standard textbook *Building Construction* (1906) show the elevation and
cross-sections of a 10-flue chimney stack serving
back-to-back houses.

Not just houses, but even major public buildings of the nineteenth century made flamboyant
use of tall chimneys, as in these examples from St

Pancras Station in London (*below*), designed by Sir
Gilbert Scott and opened in 1868. This magnificent building has recently been converted into a
luxury hotel.

A common cause of smoky chimneys was the back-pressure from other parts of the system where several fireplaces shared the same flue. Another cause, common in houses on hillsides or in windy districts, was the pressure of the wind getting down the chimney. This explains the great diversity of nineteenth-century chimney pots, with their numerous openings and little canopies. The designers were trying to prevent down-draughts and encourage cross-draughts to draw the fumes up from the fireplace. Keeping the chimney swept regularly was the best way to stop chimney fires and helped to ensure a good 'drawing' fire.

Concern about the social problem of using children as chimney sweeps produced a large philanthropic literature in the late eighteenth and early nineteenth centuries. Novels such as Charles Kingsley's *The Water Babies* raised public awareness of the problem. This is a fascinating subject, but it need not delay us here, as it is well covered by Benita Cullingford's excellent book, *British Chimney Sweeps* (2000).

Edinburgh, the capital city of Scotland, was so smoky that it was nicknamed 'Auld Reeky' (Old Smoky). From the 1740s Edinburgh had 12 appointed 'Tron-men' or official 'Custodians of the Flues' (*below*). The only approved chimney sweeps inside the Old City, they wore a broad St Andrew's bonnet as their badge of office. They did not use climbing boys, and took their name from the

Edinburgh Tron-men. Etching by John Kay, 1801.

 ALL FALL DOWN CHRISTCHURCH'S LOST CHIMNEYS

public weighing beam in front of the Tron Church where they assembled each day to await custom. If a household needed a chimney swept, a servant would be sent to summon the Tron-men.

The stone terraced housing of Edinburgh's New Town (*below*) incorporated numerous chimneys, often arranged in regular stacks, and the unregulated chimney sweeps here had no scruples about using children to get the soot out of awkward chimney stacks.

Edinburgh still has, at 24 Ardmillan Terrace (*above right*), one of the few surviving chimney sweeps' premises in Scotland. Its narrow shop window has examples of the sweep's trade, its brushes, rods and pans. The firm also deals in all types of pots, cowls, slates, tiles and lead and zinc work to repair roofs as well as chimneys.

The so-called Industrial Revolution in Britain – spanning the century from 1750 to 1850, it was rather too long to be called a revolution – created a whole new range of industrial chimneys. Coal-fired steam engines applied their motive power to a wide variety of machines and processes, and all that smoke had to be sent somewhere, preferably as far up into the sky as possible. Early industrial chimneys were sturdy square structures, with the brickwork reinforced by hoops of iron, like this restored one (*below*) at Blists Hill in the Ironbridge Gorge World Heritage site in Shropshire, the birthplace of the Industrial Revolution.

Even chimney pots could now be made of iron, like these ones (*above*), also from Ironbridge.

But round chimneys coped better with strong winds, and bricklayers rapidly developed new techniques that enabled them to build soaring graceful spires like these ones (*top right*) clustered beside an early railway in 1832. Such chimneys became typical features of the so-called 'Black Country' of

the British Midlands, where coal mines, ironworks and factories making pottery and metalwork often flourished in close proximity.

These tall industrial chimneys were masterpieces of the bricklayer's craft, substantial at the pedestal yet gradually tapering towards the top, with a lip or sill to deflect the wind and prevent down-draughts. The most common type was a double-wall barrel, with the space between left empty or filled with rubble. Though they look very solid, these chimneys were designed to be flexible and to bend in a strong wind like a tree. (A rigid stack would simply snap off at the base.) They needed regular exterior oiling to keep the rain from entering the mortar.

When maintenance was neglected they could develop a lean, usually towards the prevailing wind. When a chimney leaned more than half its top diameter, by law it had to be demolished. Bricks would be removed from the base to encourage the

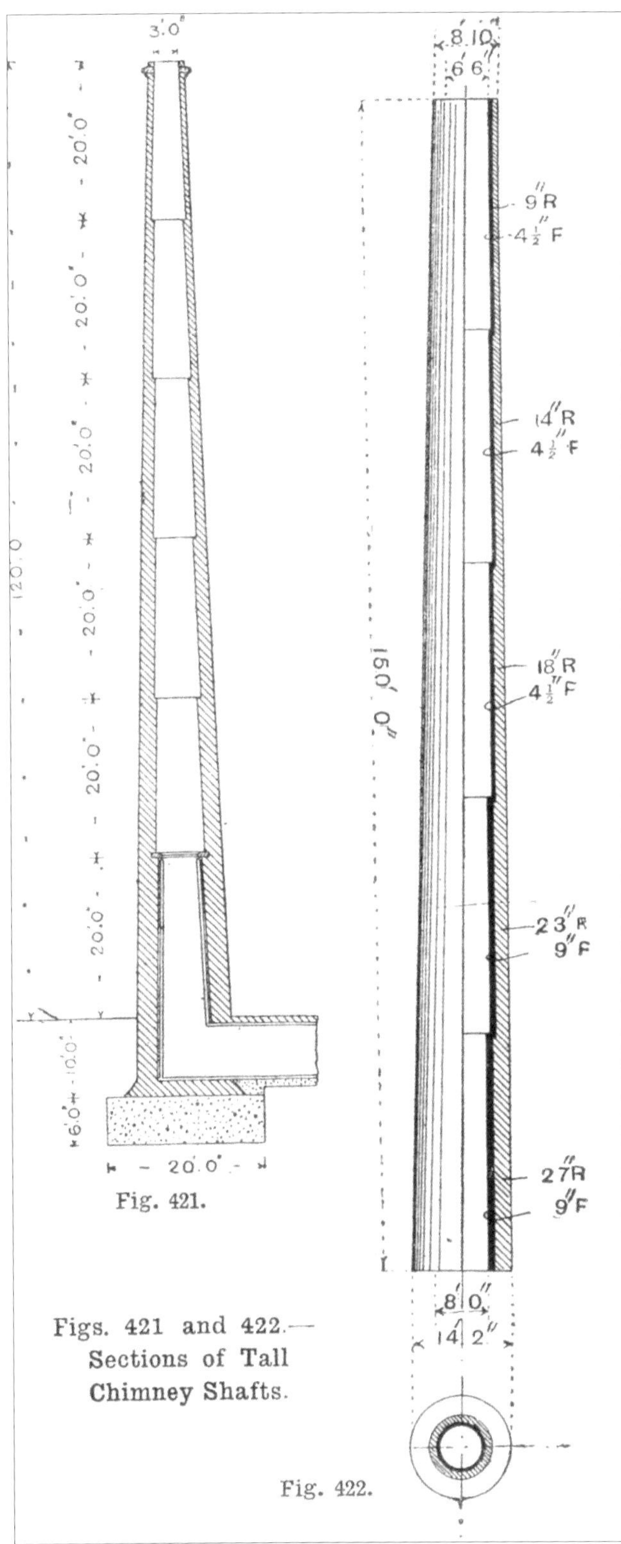

Fig. 421.

Figs. 421 and 422.— Sections of Tall Chimney Shafts.

Fig. 422.

the huge growth of Britain's urban population in the nineteenth century gave rise to acres of brick housing, which easily slid into the squalor of slums as greedy landlords and factory owners crammed

too many workers into hastily built terraces (*above*). Public health became a major issue as infectious diseases like cholera and typhoid swept through these crowded tenements in the 1840s and 1850s.

Crowded with kilns, and the tall chimneys that created a forced draught for them, the West Midlands potteries region was one of the smokiest in nineteenth-century Britain. This old

chimney to fall in a particular direction when a small explosive charge was detonated. Brick chimneys typically broke during the descent (*top right*).

The rapid expansion of industrial cities and

postcard (*opposite page*) has had various captions: 'Fresh Air from the Potteries', 'Fresh air for the Potteries', and, most telling of all, 'When the heart of the Potter rejoices'.

Not surprisingly, smog from domestic coal fires and industrial chimneys was a huge problem, along with contaminated water supplies. Smog contributed enormously to high death rates from respiratory infections, bronchitis, pneumonia and tuberculosis. London's infamous 'pea-soup' fogs, so thick that people got lost in their own neighbourhoods, were ended only in the 1960s with a total ban on open fires in the capital.

This famous engraving (*above*) by Gustav Doré of crowded tenements in London's East End, with an elevated railway in the background, has become a symbol of the adverse consequences of Britain's rapid industrialisation in the nineteenth century. Chimneys and chimney pots figure largely in this iconic image.

Escape from the dire social conditions of British industrial cities is often cited as a driver for emigration to the colonies, yet New Zealand drew most of its nineteenth-century migrants

from rural areas. Wherever they came from, they brought with them to their new land the idea of the brick chimney and its terracotta pots. It is now time to survey the history of the chimney in one of those far-flung corners of the British Empire, the planned Anglican settlement of Christchurch, capital of Canterbury province in New Zealand.

Mona Vale before
September 2010.

CHAPTER TWO

Hearth, Home and Office

Christchurch's domestic and commercial chimneys

Probably the first brick chimney in Christchurch was the one built by the Deans brothers in 1843 for their second dwelling at Putaringamotu Bush, which they renamed Riccarton after their father's farm in Scotland. (They also called the Otakaro River the Avon, from a stream on their family's Ayrshire property.) Their first home was a three-room weatherboard barn prefabricated in Wellington, to accommodate themselves and their two families of farm workers. They had bricks for a chimney, but these had to be offloaded from the whaleboat where the Avon shallowed near the present Barbadoes Street bridge. Known to the early settlers as The Bricks, this spot is now marked by a memorial cairn.

Though the barn has long since decayed and disappeared, the 1843 cottage survives at Deans Bush, on its third site. The original brick chimney has also disappeared, replaced by concrete shaped to resemble stonework.

Christchurch was a planned city, the capital of a Wakefield colony organised by the Canterbury Association and led by a young Anglo-Irish lawyer, John Robert Godley. It was intended to be a civilised Anglican settlement, complete with churches and schools, in which 'a slice of Old

House and Tents Occupied by Mr Godley. Watercolour by J. E. FitzGerald, 1852.

England' was transplanted to the Antipodes, with a familiar social hierarchy of landowners, merchants, shopkeepers, artisans and deferential agricultural labourers.

As is usual with such idealistic schemes, the reality turned out to be somewhat different. The first four chartered ships brought over 700 'Canterbury Pilgrims' to the makeshift port of Lyttelton in December 1850, soon to be followed by 15 more ships and over 3000 migrants. They included significant numbers of Wesleyans and Scottish Presbyterians, who were joined by enterprising Australian sheepfarmers nicknamed 'Shagroons',

whose wool exports saved the infant settlement from economic collapse.

Christchurch had been pegged out by the surveyors as a grid of streets on an empty plain of tussock and grass, with the flax-lined Avon River meandering through what was to become the central business district. A large open space was reserved as Hagley Park, forming a buffer between the new city and the Deans' farm at Riccarton.

Housing had to be improvised. The settlement's first medical practitioner, Dr Alfred Barker, bought a spare sail from the captain of the first migrant ship, the *Charlotte Jane*, and draped it over

a simple timber A-frame hut that he christened Studdingsail Hall (*above*). Because of the fire risk, his wife Emma had to cook their meals some distance away. This metal tube may have been the very first chimney in central Christchurch.

The first brick chimneys in the central city were probably those of the Canterbury Association's Land Office (*below left*), completed in January 1851 beside the present Worcester Street bridge, where the colonists selected their town and country sections, purchased before they left Britain.

The first domestic cottage in central Christchurch (*below*) was erected in February 1851 by George Gould, an enterprising young merchant with a bushy beard and a cheerful disposition. He had prefabricated his home in Auckland, so he only had to put it up in Armagh Street, near the Market

Land Office at Christchurch.
Watercolour by J. E. FitzGerald.

Place (later Victoria Square), and get a bricklayer to add a chimney. This cottage was later relocated to Addington.

Dr A. C. Barker photograph, 19XX.2.35, Canterbury Museum

Nearby in the Market Place, on Colombo Street (*above*), Charles Wellington Bishop built the city's first store early in 1851, and warmed it with a single fireplace and a tall chimney. He later added a little Tudor-style post office, with a smaller brick chimney.

In the 1850s and 1860s Christchurch was a straggling town of wooden cottages and shops.

Dr A. C. Barker photograph, 1958.80.29, Canterbury Museum

Dr Barker took up photography with great enthusiasm and when the first phase of the Canterbury Provincial Government Buildings had been completed he hauled his heavy wet-plate camera to the top of its tower to take a panorama of the fledgling city in 1860. This view (*bottom left*) towards the south shows several substantial brick chimneys.

Dr A. C. Barker photograph, 1944.78.202, Canterbury Museum

Looking east across the Avon River (*above*), Dr Barker has captured this group of early chimneys, mostly on buildings facing Colombo Street between Armagh and Gloucester streets. (How many of them survived the sharp earthquakes of October 1868 and June 1869, we may wonder?)

Dr A. C. Barker photograph, 1944.78.199, Canterbury Museum

This detail (*above*) of his view towards the south-west includes a sod wall in the foreground and a two-chimney cottage. The house at the right has a chimney with a projecting central course for extra lateral stability.

By the late 1860s brick chimneys were universal in Christchurch, on commercial buildings as well as domestic dwellings. This James Elsbee photograph (*below*) of the office and store of Miles & Company, grain and seed merchants in Hereford Street, is typical of the commercial buildings of the provincial period.

In the centre of this 1871 photograph (*below*), Christchurch's oldest surviving wooden commercial building (1860), now known as Shand's Emporium in Hereford Street, was originally occupied by a law firm. Next to it is the brick and stone office of the New Zealand Trust and Loan Company. Both boast chimneys.

This later Edmund Wheeler photograph (*above*), taken in the 1880s and looking the other way (east) along Hereford Street, includes a curiously top-heavy chimney halfway between Shand's and the imposing bulk of the Bank of New South Wales. Nearby chimneys have metal tubes fitted over their pots, presumably to correct smoky fireplaces.

Dr Julius von Haast, the provincial geologist and founder of Canterbury Museum, built himself this substantial brick house, Glückauf, in Avonside, with its distinctive tall pots or long toms.

Dating from 1852, Englefield on Fitzgerald Avenue is one of the city's oldest private houses still standing. It was designed by C. E. Fooks for his brother-in-law, William Guise Brittan, a leading colonist and land agent. This view of the house was made possible by the removal of trees and

shrubs in 2010 (*above*), just before the earthquake damaged its chimneys. (The 2011 earthquake finished them off.)

chimneys and Gothic spires (*above*). Vacated by the Christchurch Teachers' College in 1970, the building was later converted into apartments. Despite

Neo-Gothic was the prevailing architectural style for Christchurch's public buildings in the provincial era (1850s–1870s), with Samuel Coleridge Farr and Benjamin Mountfort as its chief exponents. Mountfort's design for the second phase of the Canterbury Provincial Government Buildings (*above*), completed in November 1865, used the chimneys as dominant features of the stone debating chamber.

S. C. Farr's design for the Normal School and Teachers' College on the corner of Kilmore and Durham streets, built in 1876, included massive

strengthening work, it suffered significant damage in 2010 and 2011.

Christchurch's Neo-Gothic 1877 railway station in Moorhouse Avenue (*below*) originally sported these stumpy brick chimneys, seen here during the royal visit of the Duke and Duchess of Cornwall in 1901.

This splendid Victorian commercial building at 244 Colombo Street (*above*), between Armagh and Gloucester streets, had matching chimneys with corbels that echoed the building's parapet.

Migrants had left Britain in search of a better life and had no wish to replicate the brick terraced housing of British industrial cities. Christchurch has just one example of such architecture, Blackheath Place in Sydenham (*above*), built by a London bricklayer in 1876. Because Blackheath had been restored and strengthened, its chimneys survived both the 2010 and 2011 earthquakes.

Most of the city's early hotels were wooden, and fire was a constant hazard, but the second generation of hotels, such as the Gladstone (*above*), on the corner of Peterborough and Durham streets, incorporated large multi-flued chimney stacks.

After a major fire in October 1888, the chimney stacks (*above*) were the only things left standing in the worst-affected wing at Sunnyside (now Hillmorton), the city's Victorian 'lunatic asylum' in Lincoln Road.

As the city matured and wooden buildings were replaced in brick and stone, flues were often incorporated into their walls with chimneys forming part of the decorative parapet, as in this 1880s view (*above*) of the first Government Life Building in Cathedral Square.

Designed by Samuel Hurst Seager, the city council's 1887 Municipal Chambers (*above*) on the corner of Oxford Terrace and Worcester Street included these four-flue chimney stacks, which survived both the 2010 and 2011 earthquakes.

Out in the expanding suburbs, wooden cottages and villas with corrugated iron roofing and verandahs had become the norm. It was a truism that 'every house had a fireplace', and most had at least two, one for the parlour and one for the kitchen, or even three, with a third for the detached lean to laundry at the rear.

Early brick chimneys were usually exterior to the framing, but by the 1880s builders tried to achieve symmetry by placing the chimney on the ridge-line of the roof. It was more economical to arrange fireplaces back to back so they could share the same flue. The basic design of the typical New Zealand chimney was very simple (*below*). A brick or concrete foundation would support a hearth at floor level, wide for wood fires and narrow for coal. A firebox with heat-resistant bricks would be topped by a barrel-vault, often supported by an iron bar from a used dray wheel. The chimney breast then narrowed to the gather, where the chimney stalk started. The flue was usually square, with a one or two-brick thickness. After 1900 there was a fashion for corner fireplaces in bedrooms, and the chimney had to be twisted through 45 degrees to emerge square with the wall or ridge-line.

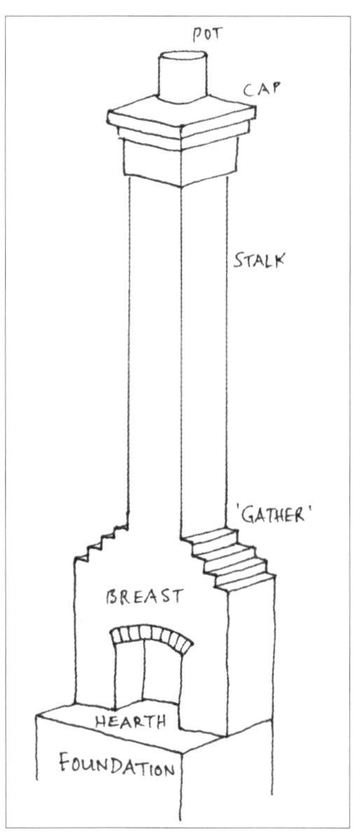

This simple single-brick-thickness stalk, common on New Zealand cottages and houses in the nineteenth century, was always vulnerable to earthquakes.

With even more decorative brickwork at the chimney cap, single-brick stalks were often top-heavy.

Older lime mortar tends to soften with age, especially if the pointing deteriorates and moisture gets into it. Rain and frost will soon weaken the side facing the prevailing wind, causing the chimney to lean.

Larger twin-flue and two-brick header and stringer chimneys were inherently stronger, and from about 1900 the use of cement mortar made them even stronger.

In the late nineteenth century steam-powered joinery factories produced an enormous range of weatherboards, ready-made doors, windows, skirting boards and mouldings, and clients could choose the detailing of their new house from a firm's catalogue. Chimney pots could also be selected from pottery catalogues. As we have seen, Homebush pots were especially popular in Christchurch in the 1880s and 1890s. This Worcester Street example (*top right*) survived the 2010 earthquake, perhaps thanks to its solidly built chimney, but it fell in 2011.

As these four photographs (*above*) testify, other Homebush pots also remained intact, until destroyed in February 2011.

 ALL FALL DOWN | Christchurch's Lost Chimneys

Other chimney pot designs were available from catalogues. This fine example (*above*) in Avonside's Gilby Street disappeared when the cottage was demolished about 2009.

This early 1900s panorama of Sydenham by Steffano Webb is full of interest for the student of housing and chimneys. Diversity prevails, with a great variety of building types and chimneys of different heights and designs. Even when the builder had erected two or three similar kitset houses, the design of the chimney was often left to the individual bricklayer's ingenuity.

This quirky Sydenham chimney top, long gone, had triangular peaks that almost concealed a diminutive plain pot.

On the other side of town, in a more affluent suburb with larger sections, is this extensive tile-roofed 1890s wooden house (*above*) with splendid brick chimneys and Homebush pots. Remarkably, it survived the 2010 earthquake unscathed, but the chimneys fell in February 2011.

At another extreme, some chimneys were strictly practical, with no pretence to elegance. This rebuilt example (*above*) from Peterborough Street fell victim to the 2010 earthquake.

Brick chimneys were the dominant vertical features of these early state houses built in Sydenham (*above*) under the 1908 Workers' Dwellings Act. Like the second generation of 1930s state houses, the designs were subtly varied to avoid any appearance of uniformity.

In the 1880s there was a fashion for disguising brick chimneys with a smooth stucco finish. This also gave scope for more elegant cornices, as in this example (*above left*) from a shop at the corner of Worcester Street and Fitzgerald Avenue. This chimney survived the September 2010 shake, but not that of 2011.

Likewise, these two examples (*above right*) from the central city are no more.

These two Addington villas (*opposite page, bottom right*) are typical of many larger Christchurch suburban houses in the early 1900s, and are very similar to the Waltham house in which I spent my childhood. Each chimney would serve two back-to-back fireplaces. Though they survived both major earthquakes, these chimneys were taken down after February 2011.

Domestic chimneys in early twentieth-century Christchurch varied according to whether they were designed by a bricklayer or an architect. The latter produced some impressive chimneys for wealthier clients, and even for themselves. These were the fine chimneys on Robert England's house in Bealey Avenue (*above*), in the nostalgic Old English-Tudor style popular at the time. Sad to say, this fine old house collapsed in the February 2011 earthquake.

The Pyne family residence at 82 Bealey Avenue (*top right*) originally had these unusual top-heavy brick chimneys. Their removal many years ago probably helped Eliza's Manor, as it is now known, to survive in February 2011.

Mona Vale (1905) (*above*) was designed by J. C. Madison for Annie Townend, daughter of the runholder G. H. Moore, with no expense spared. Its chimneys were badly damaged in September 2010 and again in 2011, but are to be restored.

The Rhodes Memorial Convalescent Home on Cashmere Hill once boasted a remarkable collection of brick chimneys, complete with metal modifications to cope with the prevailing easterly wind and occasional down-draughts from the hillside above. Designed by Frederick Strouts, the home was opened in 1886 as a memorial to the pre-Adamite Canterbury settler Robert Heaton Rhodes (1815–84). With his brothers William and George he had pioneered sheep farming on Banks Peninsula before the arrival of the Canterbury Association settlers, and later became wealthy from the subdivision of cheap land on the Canterbury Plains. He was a major benefactor of the Christchurch Cathedral, donating the cost of its tower and bells. The cathedral's spire was a memorial gift from the family of his younger brother George, who died in 1865. Robert's namesake son, better known in Canterbury as Sir Heaton Rhodes (1861–1956), MP for Ellesmere and cabinet minister, was closely involved in the management of the Rhodes Home for most of his adult life, and once complained that

in spite of its numerous fireplaces the building was difficult to keep warm, with its tall ceilings and wide hospital-style corridors.

Most of the chimneys were taken down in the 1960s as gas and electricity replaced coal fires in the Home, and the September 2010 earthquake damaged the remaining ones. Expensive external repairs had just been completed when the February 2011 earthquake severely damaged the building, collapsing walls and bay windows. The whole structure was demolished in March 2011 and the site cleared.

The Rhodes Home had been the first large building on Cashmere Hill. With the collapse of the Christchurch Cathedral spire and the loss of its bells, and the demolition of the Nurse Maude District Nursing building in Madras Street, the February 2011 earthquake has deprived Christchurch of most of its major benefactions by the pioneering Rhodes family.

Los Angeles in Fendalton Road (*above*), designed by J. S. Guthrie, is New Zealand's first example of the California bungalow style. Its riverstone chimneys did not enjoy the shaking they had to endure in September 2010 and have been taken down.

Cecil Wood was Christchurch's leading exponent of Georgian Revival in the inter-war period. Here (*above*) is his finest example, the Weston House (1923) in Park Terrace. The bricks came from the Glenmore Brickworks in Port Hills Road.

Wood also designed the second Bishopscourt (1926), further along Park Terrace (*above*), in a style evocative of American Colonial Georgian, with chimneys to match.

Modernist and Art Deco styles of the 1930s and 1940s were as popular in Christchurch as in other New Zealand towns (most famously Napier after the February 1931 earthquake). Flat roofs made these houses cold in winter, and chimneys were still necessary in the absence of central heating. This stylish chimney in Papanui (*above*)

included a cover above the front door. Sadly it did not survive the 2011 earthquake.

In this example (*above*) the chimney has been painted to echo the design on the corner of the house.

Stucco or rough-cast coatings were also favoured during the 1920s and 1930s. These fine examples (*above*) were on Cashmere Hill.

The Art Deco style could include highly individual designs, like this surviving example in Ryan Street, Linwood (*above*).

These stylish Fendalton chimneys (*above*) both survived the earthquakes and aftershocks. The one on the right evokes the Italian-style tile-tent chimney with a rather diminutive pot.

From the same period these Opawa Road chimneys (*above*) survived both earthquakes intact.

Many of Christchurch's suburban bungalows of the 1920s and 1930s, whether in brick or weatherboard, have distinctive chimneys that include the use of darker knapped bricks (*above*).

This chimney (*above left*) in Riccarton was broken at the roof-line on 4 September 2010 and had to be taken down.

Another fashion in the inter-war years and the 1940s was the use of red or dark grey volcanic stone from Banks Peninsula, as in this example from Bryndwr (*above right*), which survived the 2010 earthquake intact but was later taken down.

This straight-sided St Albans chimney (*left*) did not.

Perhaps the most interesting fashion of the years between the world wars was the inclusion in darker bricks of a reversed

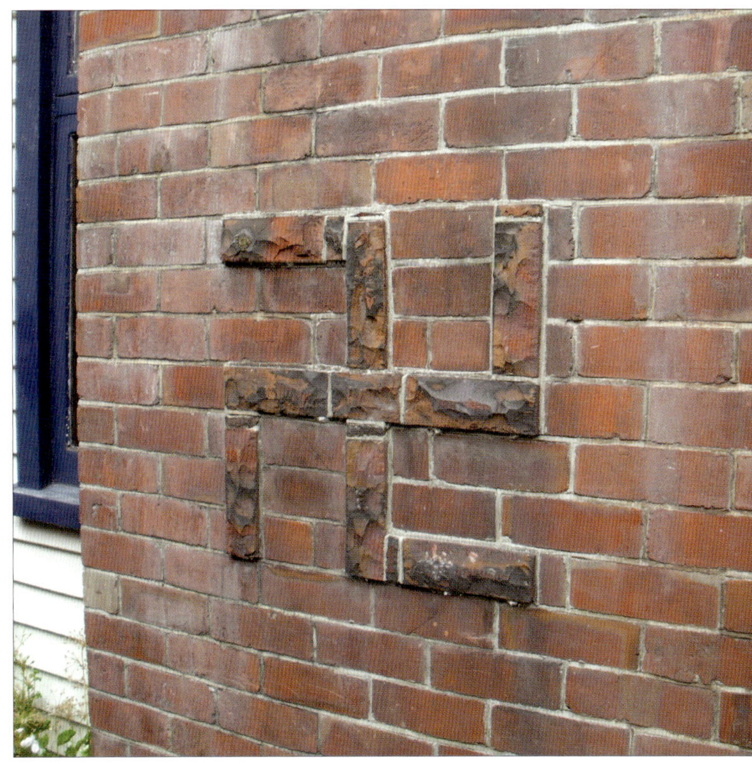

swastika pattern. The right-handed swastika is
of course familiar as the symbol of Hitler's Nazi
Germany, turned 45 degrees, but the square reverse
swastika is an ancient Buddhist symbol originating
in India, from where it spread to China, Tibet and
Japan. It is the character for 10,000 (*jumanji*) and
signifies good luck.

This fine example (*above*) on the corner of
Rossall Street and Merivale Lane was a familiar
sight for motorists coming into the city from the
north-west until it was demolished after the chim-

ney suffered major damage
in September 2010.

Though the top of
this chimney in Bryndwr
(*left*) fell in the 2010
earthquake, its reversed
swastika has been
retained.

This example survives in Linwood. It would
be interesting to know more about these chimneys
and whether the idea for the peace symbol came
from the owner, the architect or the builder. They
may represent a desire for world peace after the
carnage of the First World War, which was hope-
fully called in the 1920s 'the war to end all wars'.

Unlike some New Zealand cities, Christchurch
had a strong tradition of providing city council
rental flats. Among the first were these (*above*),

dating from 1938, in Barnett Terrace beside Sydenham Park, with English-looking long-tom chimney pots. These were removed some years ago as possible earthquake risks.

Vale. Homebush pots surmounted this four-flue stack on a house in Peterborough Street (*top left*), now gone, and the fine three-flue stack (*bottom left*) was in Dyers Pass Road on Cashmere Hill.

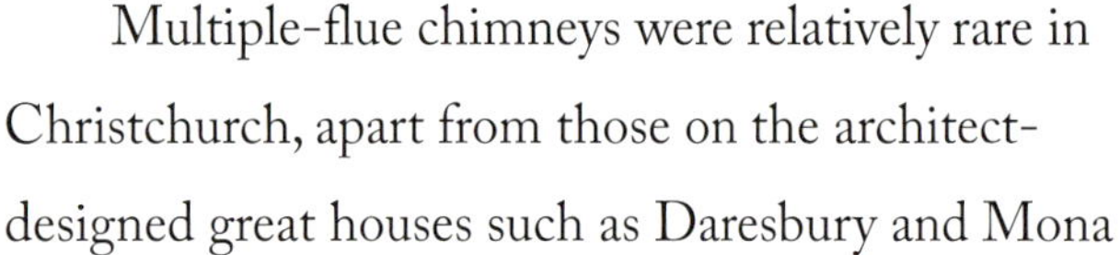

Multiple-flue chimneys were relatively rare in Christchurch, apart from those on the architect-designed great houses such as Daresbury and Mona

From the 1930s, Christchurch's domestic chimneys included numerous examples on state houses (*above and opposite top*), constructed by the Department of Housing Construction and made available to working-class families on easy mortgages through the State Advances Corporation, as part of the first Labour government's welfare state programme.

 ALL FALL DOWN | CHRISTCHURCH'S LOST CHIMNEYS

Deliberately varied in size and design, state houses were compact, economical and well built. Leading architects were invited to submit designs according to the government's specifications, and over 400 were received. In Christchurch, the England brothers' designs were among those accepted, and they favoured the English cottage style, combining brick and weatherboards with a tile roof. Chimneys were mostly very simple brick affairs, with various amounts of stucco to add individual touches.

Christchurch suburbs, especially in the northwest and east of the city (*above*), expanded rapidly in the 'baby-boom' era following the Second World War. Many streets were built by development companies that offered a limited range of basic designs at a reasonable cost, like this standard 1960s Burnside bungalow (*right*). Its plain chimney survived both the 2010 and 2011 quakes.

In the 1950s and 1960s builders copied the best features of state house construction on a larger scale, and produced the standard brick-veneer concrete-tile house with plain brick chimneys that may be found in every Christchurch suburb of that era. The chimneys were often reinforced with steel rods, and many survived the 2010 earthquake.

Concrete-block and Summerhill stone flats or units were also popular in the 1960s and 1970s. Many of these reinforced chimneys, too, were unaffected by the 2010 earthquake (*bottom left and below*).

Among post-war architects, Miles Warren pioneered a stripped-down simplified Modernist style with a distinctive Canterbury look, using concrete block construction. His Dorset Street flats (1956–57) (*above*) were the first of a long line of such flats and houses, much copied by other architects.

Chimneys are a more dominant feature of this block of flats in Oxford Terrace (*above*).

The tall brick chimneys of these Merivale flats (*above*) survived the 2010 shake but not that of 2011.

Christchurch's flat coastal site on a former swamp (*above*) makes it prone to temperature inversion on frosty mornings, and the discharge of thousands of coal fires tended to hang about to form smog, as seen in this 1970s photo.

Clean-air regulations became progressively stricter from the 1980s, finally culminating in a ban on open fires. In recent decades new chimneys in Christchurch have been designed for log-burners rather than open fires. Many older chimneys have also sprouted small metal flues (*above*).

But the 2010 earthquake often shattered the

brickwork, leaving the metal tube standing by itself (*left*). Many chimneys that had been slightly damaged in September were finally wrecked by the aftershocks on Boxing Day or by the devastating earthquake of 22 February 2011.

Newer chimneys had a much better chance of survival, and we shall meet some examples of these in the Epilogue.

Boilerhouse chimney,
University of Canterbury.

CHAPTER THREE

Stacks, Pipes and Smokers

Christchurch's industrial chimneys

Christchurch developed in the second half of the nineteenth century as the market town for Canterbury Province. Its economy was shaped by the agricultural and pastoral products of innumerable small farms on the plains and the extensive sheep runs of the high country. Wool was the mainstay of the fledgling economy, followed by wheat, then meat and dairying. New technologies, especially refrigeration, revolutionised the export sector from the 1880s, enabling shiploads of wool, frozen lamb and mutton to be sent more quickly to British markets, along with butter and cheese from the 1890s.

Quite apart from the railways and the gasworks, industrial chimneys must have made Christchurch a remarkably smoky place in the late nineteenth century. In the decades preceding the First World War the city probably had New Zealand's largest manufacturing sector, before being overtaken by Auckland and Wellington, and remained an innovative sector in the twentieth century, pioneering plastics and electrical goods. Early Christchurch industries relied on coal-fired steam engines for their motive power, and furnaces needed tall chimneys both to provide adequate draught and to disperse their smoke. A great variety of tall brick chimneys used to be a familiar part of the Christchurch townscape, especially south of Moorhouse Avenue, and in the industrial suburbs of Hornby and Woolston. But now they have all gone, mostly demolished in the 1920s and 1930s as electricity became more readily available.

John Anderson's first forge was beside the Avon River near The Bricks, but in the 1860s he built his main foundry in Cashel Street on a site now in the heart of the city's central business district, facing the City Mall (*above*). Photographs of early New Zealand industrial chimneys are surprisingly rare, but this one shows Anderson's Cashel Street foundry just before it was demolished when he moved to larger premises about 1879.

Anderson's must have been the first proper industrial chimney in Christchurch, but it was soon joined by those of the early breweries, tanneries and flour mills. Most of that flour was turned into bread and biscuits, and Aulsebrook's became a household name in Australasia for its biscuits and crackers well into the twentieth century.

The Belfast Freezing Works (*top*), and its rival the Canterbury Meat Company (*above*), both had massive brick chimneys. Belfast's was one of the largest industrial chimneys in the province.

The animal skins went to the tanneries at Woolston and, once processed, moved on to a number of boot and shoe factories. In the 1890s Christchurch was New Zealand's leading centre for footwear manufacture.

Soap- and candle-makers were also numerous in early Christchurch, with neighbours often complaining about the smell and smoke. Clothing and knitwear formed another Christchurch speciality, with major companies like the Kaiapoi Woollen Manufacturing Company and Lane Walker Rudkin employing hundreds of workers. Engineering works such as Anderson's, J. & A. P. Scott, P. & D. Duncan and later Andrews & Beaven not only made a wide range of agricultural machinery but also steam locomotives and coal ranges. Anderson's even manufactured such large items as boilers, dredges and the steelwork for railway bridges and viaducts.

Timber mills and joinery factories were numerous in Christchurch, producing kitset houses, doors and window-frames as well as furniture. At least they could use their off-cuts to help fire their boilers. The lower slopes of the Port Hills had thick deposits of loess clay, suitable for making bricks and pipes, and the brickworks of Port Hills Road and Centaurus Road were among the last survivors of tall industrial brick chimneys in the city.

M. Moseley's *Illustrated Guide to Christchurch and Neighbourhood*, published in 1885, included a number of ink drawings of its advertisers' premises, many of which boasted tall chimneys. This is Mitchell's Zealandia Carpet Factory in Ferry Road (*top opposite page*), the first such factory in New Zealand.

The early settlers liked to liven up their bread and cheese with pickles and relish; Christchurch was a major pickle producer in the 1880s. The

Maclean Pickle and Preserving Company Ltd (*above*) stood in St Asaph Street, near Montreal Street.

Crompton's Crown Iron Works in Armagh Street made thousands of colonial ovens and coal ranges in the nineteenth century, and judging by the number of chimneys in this illustration (*right*) must have been a major source of smoke pollution as well.

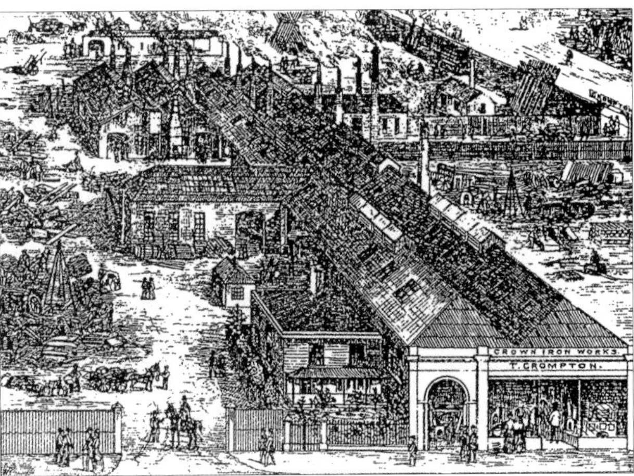

Scott Brothers' Atlas Foundry in lower Manchester Street manufactured the first New Zealand-made steam locomotives, as well as a wide range of metal products, including coal ranges.

Kempthorne & Prosser's Chemical Works at Hornby (*above*), shown here in the 1920s, produced large quantities of fertiliser for Canterbury farms.

In the 1870s Christchurch had been New Zealand's least healthy city, with high death rates from typhoid and other infectious diseases that were blamed on cross-contamination between water wells and cesspits. The Drainage Board built New Zealand's first underground sewerage system in the 1880s, with this pumping station at the corner of Tuam Street and Mathesons Road (*above*). The system was electrified in the 1930s and the chimney demolished, but the buildings survive. This photo appeared in the *Weekly Press* in 1897.

These chimneys, on Aulsebrook's premises (*above*) at the corner of Montreal and St Asaph streets, were made redundant by the electrification of the plant in the 1920s.

Prisk and Savage had a small brickworks on Port Hills Road in the 1890s, seen here (*above*) in about 1915 with the Glenmore works in the distance. There was good brick-making clay at the foot of the Port Hills, and at one time there were at least seven brickworks dotted between Avoca Valley and Bowenvale.

The Glenmore Brick & Tile Manufacturing Company was established on Port Hills Road below Murray Aynsley spur in 1901, and at first had two kilns with these distinctive tall brick chimneys (*above*). The original company went into liquidation in 1942 and was revived by Aldersons of Dunedin in 1946. After 1965 it became a subsidiary of McSkimmings Industries, and was the last remaining Christchurch brickworks until its closure in the 1980s.

The Glenmore Brickworks specialised in making hollow constructional tiles that could be filled with concrete or cement grouting around reinforcing rods. This page from their 1930s catalogue advertises 'Quake-Proof Chimneys', claiming that they were 'Easy and quick to build, and will never shake down'. However, very few of them appear to have been built, as most Christchurch chimneys of the 1930s and 1940s continued to be traditional brick structures.

Another early brickworks was this one (*above*) in Heathcote Valley, seen here in 1912, later replaced by Henry Wigram's maltworks.

Luke Adams started his pottery works in Sydenham in the 1880s, and trained his sons to help him make a wide range of demijohns, butter jars, teapots, jugs and ornamental ware. One son invented a miniature press to make toy bricks known as Kiddibricks, which were still being made when the plant closed in the 1960s.

A tall smoking industrial chimney like that of the Islington Works of the Christchurch Meat Company (*above*) could be a useful landmark on the flat Canterbury Plains.

Also eye-catching was the Wood Brothers' flour mill in Wise Street, Addington (*above*). The tall building survived the 2011 earthquake, but was demolished in haste lest it collapse in an aftershock and damage other nearby buildings. The even taller chimney had been demolished many years earlier.

James Goss was a leading builder, contractor and timber merchant in late nineteenth-century Christchurch, with a joinery factory and its smoky chimney (*opposite page, top left*) on the corner

PhotoCD 13, IMG0013, Christchurch City Libraries

of Durham and Peterborough streets (now the Christchurch Casino carpark).

PhotoCD 6, IMG0027, Christchurch City Libraries

The city's leading department store, J. Ballantyne & Co, had its own steam furniture factory and upholstering works in Tuam Street in 1900 (*bottom left*).

PhotoCD 13, IMG0006, Christchurch City Libraries

Grummitt & White's clothing factory stood at 115 St Asaph Street from the 1870s until the early 1900s, and employed large numbers of women. These splendid chimneys (*above*) suggest that there was at least some attempt to keep them warm in the winter months.

Christchurch Star

The Addington Railway Workshops (*above*) were powered by five former locomotive steam engines in the boiler house beside the water tower, with their combined smoke discharged through the two plain metal chimneys. The 1883 water tower survives in the midst of a megastore shopping complex; everything else in this photo disappeared in the 1990s.

Canterbury Area Health Board Collection, Canterbury Historical Association Collection, 2000.198.782, Canterbury Museum

Christchurch's first brewery was founded in 1854 by J. Hamilton Ward and A. C. Croft. Its handsome brick malthouse and bottling plant near the Fitzgerald Avenue bridge (*above*) survived the demise of the company and were used by a variety of tenants, including the Crichton Cobbers gym and Pickwick's Trading Company, only to be demolished after it was badly damaged on 22 February 2011.

The lower Heathcote River in Woolston was used by early wool-scouring companies, one of which developed into the Davis Glue and Gelatine factory, seen here (*top right*). The effluent from such activities, and from the tanneries, seriously polluted the river until stricter legislation prompted dramatic improvements in the 1990s.

One of the tallest chimneys in the inner city belonged to Christchurch Hospital (*above*), at the intersection of Riccarton and Hagley avenues, seen here in the 1930s looming over the administration block. The 1894 Nurses' Home is on the right. None of these buildings exists today, the last demolished in the 1980s to make way for the new hospital and medical school.

The city's most interesting collection of industrial chimneys was to be found at the gasworks on Moorhouse Avenue (*opposite page, top*), at the north end of Waltham Road. This view from the 1930s includes no fewer than seven substantial brick chimneys.

This fine brick chimney (*opposite page, centre left*) beside the old Retort House at the Christchurch Gasworks was demolished in the 1950s.

 ALL FALL DOWN | CHRISTCHURCH'S LOST CHIMNEYS

The chimney on the right was the tallest at the gasworks, but it was not designed to carry away smoke. Instead it released billows of steam whenever the red-hot cooked coal from the gas-producing process was quenched with cold water to produce coke. Forced to close by Brierley Investments Limited, the Gas Company ceased production in 1982, the gasholders were dismantled and the whole site cleared for redevelopment as an 'industrial park' in the 1990s.

Not many brick industrial chimneys survived the inter-war years because most Christchurch factories converted to electricity and steel pipes were

much cheaper for those who still needed a chimney. Bricklayers skilled in the art of constructing very tall chimneys, who must have been numerous in the nineteenth century, were becoming very rare in New Zealand.

By far the best-known (or most notorious) chimney in early twentieth-century central Christchurch was that of the city council's rubbish destructor (*above*). This, with its smoke plume, appears towards the bottom of this very first aerial photograph of the city, taken by Leslie Hinge in January 1918. There's an interesting story behind this chimney, whose ovens not only burned Christchurch's rubbish for over 30 years but also generated electricity and heated the city's first tepid baths.

Electricity came to Canterbury in the late 1870s. Miles & Company were agents for the Gülcher generating system, which first lit up the Lyttelton wharves in 1882. The city council was keen to use electricity for street lighting, but already had a long-term contract with the Gas Company for this purpose. When the tender came up for renewal in 1892 the council amended its

terms to include electricity, but the only tenders for electricity were far too expensive and the Gas Company won another seven-year contract.

Several Christchurch factories and department stores switched to electricity, using small oil- or gas-fired engines connected to a dynamo and storage batteries. But street lighting would need a much larger and more reliable source of power. The city council began to explore potential generating sites in the Canterbury foothills, including the Waimakariri Gorge. The government finally selected Lake Coleridge as the best site for

power generation and started construction of a power station there in 1911.

In the meantime, someone had the bright idea of burning the city's rubbish and using the heat to drive a steam-powered generator. This was a common practice in many British cities, so the technology was readily available. A site was found in Armagh Street and a rubbish destructor with two large ovens was built in 1901–02. The brick chimney (*above*) stood 45.7m (150ft) tall, rivalling the cathedral spire (63m) as the tallest structure in central Christchurch.

Unlike the much-admired spire, however, the destructor chimney merely added to the winter smog, and became known as 'the tower of stench'. Apart from domestic rubbish, the destructor also consumed the city's unsold fish and butchers' offal. The Customs Department often sent items on which duty had not been paid, including tobacco and one memorable consignment of several tons of illegally caught 'mutton birds' (sooty shearwater). Life for the workers at the furnaces was not only hot and dirty but at times risky, when the occasional live cartridge exploded. In 1919 a worker who had returned unscathed from the First World War was wounded in the shoulder by a bullet flying out of the furnace.

The next step was to make use of all this abundant heat. In March 1902 the city council commissioned a report on electricity generation and an Australian company won the tender to build two steam boilers, each of which would drive a 100kW generator. Soon after its completion, the plant was handed over to the newly formed Municipal Electricity Department.

But that was not the only use for the destructor. Citizens had been lobbying the council for years to provide tepid baths, as the Avon was too shallow for swimming and pools filled with artesian water were icy cold. Teachers were concerned at the large numbers of children who never learned to swim. Now the council had the means to heat such a pool, and the Christchurch Municipal Tepid Baths ('the Teps') were opened in May 1908 on an adjacent site further east along Armagh Street. They were later replaced by the Centennial Pool, which in turn has become the Centennial Recreation and Sport Centre.

Hydro-electric power from Lake Coleridge came to the city in 1915, and the opening of the Waitaki hydro station in 1935 finally made the destructor's generator redundant. The council decided to dispose of its rubbish at landfill sites in Bexley and Burwood and the destructor's ovens finally shut down in 1938. After being surrounded by scaffolding (*below*), the chimney was carefully demolished, brick by brick, in 1939, removing a city landmark but also ending 37 years of smog and stench.

 ALL FALL DOWN Christchurch's Lost Chimneys

Many other brick industrial chimneys fell victim to the advent of electricity. This remarkable 1920s photograph (*above*) shows the 1883 graving dock chimney at Lyttelton being pulled down, after the pumps had been converted from steam to electricity.

Much later, in 1974, this large brickworks chimney in Centaurus Road was taken down (*top and centre right*). The Murphy brickworks in Centaurus Road, Beckenham, had been founded as the Farnley Brick & Tile Works in 1875 by brothers John and William Austin and Henry Kirk, who invested in a Hoffman kiln in 1880. The business was later taken over by Horsley & Company, before they in turn were bought out by the Murphy brothers.

In 1983 demolition began on the 1931 chimney of the builders Dodge Bros Ltd at the corner of Bealey and Fitzgerald avenues (*above*). Danny Coffey is seen here knocking out the bricks.

Now closed, the Lane Walker Rudkin knitwear factory (*below left*) made clothing for generations of Christchurch residents, including Canterbury sports apparel. In its heyday it was one of the city's largest employers of women.

Christchurch has some fine, if visually boring, examples of the modern industrial chimney. The University of Canterbury (*above left*) opted for a coal-fired central heating system when it moved from its town site (now the Arts Centre) to the suburb of Ilam in the 1970s, and this tall chimney still wafts smoke over the district in the winter months.

The former North Canterbury Hospital Board built this severely plain concrete chimney for its new laundry plant in Hillmorton, to serve all the Christchurch hospitals (*above right*).

This plaster-board factory in Woolston (*above*) now has one of the city's tallest steel chimney stacks.

There is still a large chemical works at Hornby (*above*), but clean-air regulations now require sophisticated filtration systems to prevent the escape of noxious gases into the environment.

Sydenham still has a few small furnaces with plain metal tube chimneys like this one (*left*).

Antigua Street almost has a tall-chimney precinct, with those of the hospital and the Canterbury Brewery near each other (*below left*). One block further east there was another tall concrete chimney on Montreal Street until it was taken down after the February 2011 earthquake.

These modern pipes and stacks all survived the 2010 and 2011 earthquakes, but it is doubtful whether any of their brick predecessors would have fared as well. Perhaps we should count our blessings. If Christchurch's tall brick Victorian chimney stacks had still been around, most would have collapsed, unleashing tons of bricks onto their immediate surroundings.

Papanui Road, February 2011.

CHAPTER FOUR

The Big Shakes of 2010 and 2011

Together with thousands of other fellow citizens of the Garden City, we were woken at 4.36am on Saturday 4 September 2010 by a loud approaching rumble. We live not far from a railway line, but this was no freight train: it sounded more like several express trains approaching at speed. Then the shaking started. 'This is a big one!' was my understatement of the year as we stumbled across the bedroom to take shelter in the doorway. As we held onto the doorframe to stay upright, the noise intensified. From outside came a general roar, like a strong nor'west gale, while inside we could hear things falling and crashing throughout the house. We had to shout to make ourselves heard.

The shaking seemed to go on for minutes, but time had slowed down. Though we did not know it until later, the first big shake lasted only 30 seconds, but it was magnitude 7.1, in global terms a 'major earthquake', the same strength as the Haiti earthquake at the start of 2010, which had claimed an estimated 230,000 lives. Amazingly, the electricity still worked, so we turned the lights on as we picked our way carefully along the hall, over tumbled books and ornaments. The kitchen floor was littered with broken glass, and the dishwasher drawers and several cupboard doors were hanging

open. The fridge had deposited half its contents onto our imitation Turkish rug. Bottles of wine had bounced but not broken.

Then came the first big aftershock and the lights went out. Like most people, we put on more clothes and went back to bed to keep warm, for it was a cold morning. We listened to an old transistor radio, and smiled at Radio New Zealand National's unwitting selection of 'Good Vibrations' among its all-night music. We wondered if the Alpine Fault had ruptured at last, but as more reports came in it looked as if the epicentre had been out on the Canterbury Plains, somewhere near Darfield. Using our cellphones we were able to check that family and friends were safe and well, though shaken and fearful.

Aftershocks came thick and fast as we went over our disaster-preparedness list. Thanks to the constant TV reminders by the Earthquake Commission (EQC), we had ample stocks of food and batteries, and a barbecue with half a tank of gas, but water might be a problem: we had emptied our Y2K water containers and forgotten to refill them. Luckily there was enough water in the kitchen kettle to pour into a saucepan and heat on a camping-gas burner for hot drinks. There was plenty of juice and milk in the fridge, but how long would the power stay off? Meat in the freezer would soon start to defrost. The radio told us not to flush the loo as the sewerage pumps were all out of action.

At first light I went outside to assess the damage. Our greatest earthquake fear had failed to materialise. The lounge fireplace had a tall brick chimney, and if it had fallen back onto the roof it would have crashed through the tiles and into the house. I had always been meaning to secure it with metal struts, but somehow it hadn't seemed a high priority. After all, this wasn't Wellington. Amazingly, both our chimneys were still standing. But on closer inspection I found that the lounge chimney had broken off at roof level (*below*) and had shifted a few centimetres towards the gutter. There appeared to be just one brick holding it up.

Our neighbour said it looked hazardous and should come down. A single push sent the chimney crashing to the ground, demolishing a trellis fence on the way (*above*). Inside it were six rusty reinforcing rods.

Electricity was restored to our street midmorning, and with the phone working again a semblance of normality started to return. Neighbours were soon inspecting each other's houses and exchanging earthquake stories. After we had cleaned up the mess in the kitchen, and discovered ornaments that had bounced right across the lounge, my two teenage sons started to help me break up the fallen chimney. This was hard labour, as the chimney appeared to have been filled with concrete between the flue and the brickwork.

The following day, a calm sunny Sunday, we went for a walk around nearby blocks. The most obvious and visible damage in every street was to the chimneys. Some were still upright, but only just, as the bricks had been shaken apart. In between collapsed chimneys there were survivors that looked perfectly intact. Plain stucco chimneys from the 1970s seemed to have fared pretty well.

Perhaps they had been reinforced, like ours. As
I took photos (*below and right and following two
pages*) in the spring sunshine, I resolved to write
this book. The earthquake had drawn our attention
to chimneys as never before.

The next day, driving into town to inspect the damage there, I was delighted to see that one of my personal favourites was still standing, at the corner of Rossall and Rhodes streets. This was a tall yellow-brick chimney with a distinctive curved canopy instead of a chimney pot. Though the matching brick wall had collapsed, the chimney was still there (*below*).

Much of the inner city had been cordoned off, and the army had arrived to help the police deter looters. Here were checkpoints and army vehicles, in peaceful Christchurch, of all places. I was able to walk through Victoria Square, where nothing appeared to have been damaged, and could see the cathedral still standing, but bricks were littering the streets where parts of older buildings had fallen away. Cranes were already busy. I had no idea there were so many cranes in Christchurch. At the northern end of Cranmer Square the Neo-Gothic former Normal School had suffered extensive damage to its gables and corner octagon, and had

lost its chimneys. These massive brick and cement objects were now sitting incongruously on the footpath (*below*).

The Durham Street Methodist Church had suffered extensive cracking and had lost masonry from its parapet. At the rear, an elderly brick chimney was still standing but had been shaken apart and was later taken down (*opposite page above left*).

The Provincial Government Buildings, Benjamin Mountfort's masterpiece, were still standing. Recent earthquake strengthening had done its job well, and the great stone debating chamber, the finest Gothic Revival interior in the southern hemisphere, appeared to be intact.

Samuel Hurst Seager's elegant 1880s redbrick municipal building beside the Avon had lost some of its tiles, but the chimneys were still in place (*bottom*).

The Arts Centre, formerly the town site of

the University of Canterbury, where I had been a student, written my doctoral thesis and delivered my very first lecture in the Great Hall, had suffered extensive superficial damage to its gables, and the Clock Tower on Worcester Boulevard was badly damaged, but the rest of it looked fine and reparable.

But other buildings had suffered major damage, especially the churches. St John's in Latimer Square looked as if a bomb had hit it, and the splendid columned frontage of the Oxford Terrace Baptist Church was badly cracked and in danger of collapse. The former Methodist Church on Papanui Road in Merivale had lost so many bricks from its tower that the spire had to be removed by a crane and it now sat on the ground, looking somewhat startled and out of place.

Many brick buildings in Sydenham had been badly damaged, including this notable 1880s shop on the corner of Sandyford and Colombo streets (*below*), which later had to be demolished.

Perched precariously on its sagging roof was this odd decorative feature which looked like a chimney but had no flue or pots (*below*). Perhaps it had been capped at some early date when the fireplace was blocked up, or had it been just a decorative feature all along?

As the aftershocks from the September 2010 earthquake diminished, the rubble from collapsed brick frontages was cleared away and life began to feel more usual. Everyone was amazed and pleased that nobody had been killed. The expensive earthquake strengthening of major heritage buildings like the Anglican Cathedral and the Canterbury Museum had apparently paid off.

Newspaper reports after the first major shocks of September 2010 estimated that over 17,000 brick chimneys had fallen in Christchurch, or were damaged beyond repair. In October the EQC announced a scheme, in conjunction with the Energy Efficiency and Conservation Authority (EECA), that offered homeowners with significantly damaged chimneys the opportunity to replace their open fires or old log-burners with heat pumps, gas space heaters or approved wood or pellet burners. The householder would pay an excess of only $200 on each appliance; the EQC would meet the cost of the appliance and its installation.

This enlightened idea seemed likely to solve Christchurch's historic smog problem at one stroke. The city council and Environment Canterbury had long since given notice that open fires and smoky old log-burners were on the way out. Open fires had been banned for two years, and the air was a great deal cleaner as a result – not perfect on still frosty nights, but vastly better for asthmatics. It is said that every cloud has a silver lining. This earthquake had a silver bullet for the smog problem.

The earthquake marked the end of an era for the city's chimney heritage. Already many streets were looking strangely different. Where, sometimes for more than a century, chimneys had delighted the eye, there were now bare flat roof-lines. This was especially noticeable in streets with underground wiring and without the usual Kiwi forest of power poles. It looked as if a large bomb had levelled everything but the houses.

By late January 2011 it was reported that more than 30,000 of the 175,000 claims lodged with EQC were for chimney or fireplace damage (*see map, opposite page*). Seventy per cent of claimants were opting for heat pumps to replace their old open fires.

A few brick chimneys were being rebuilt by owners anxious to retain the authentic aesthetic appearance of their heritage properties. After all,

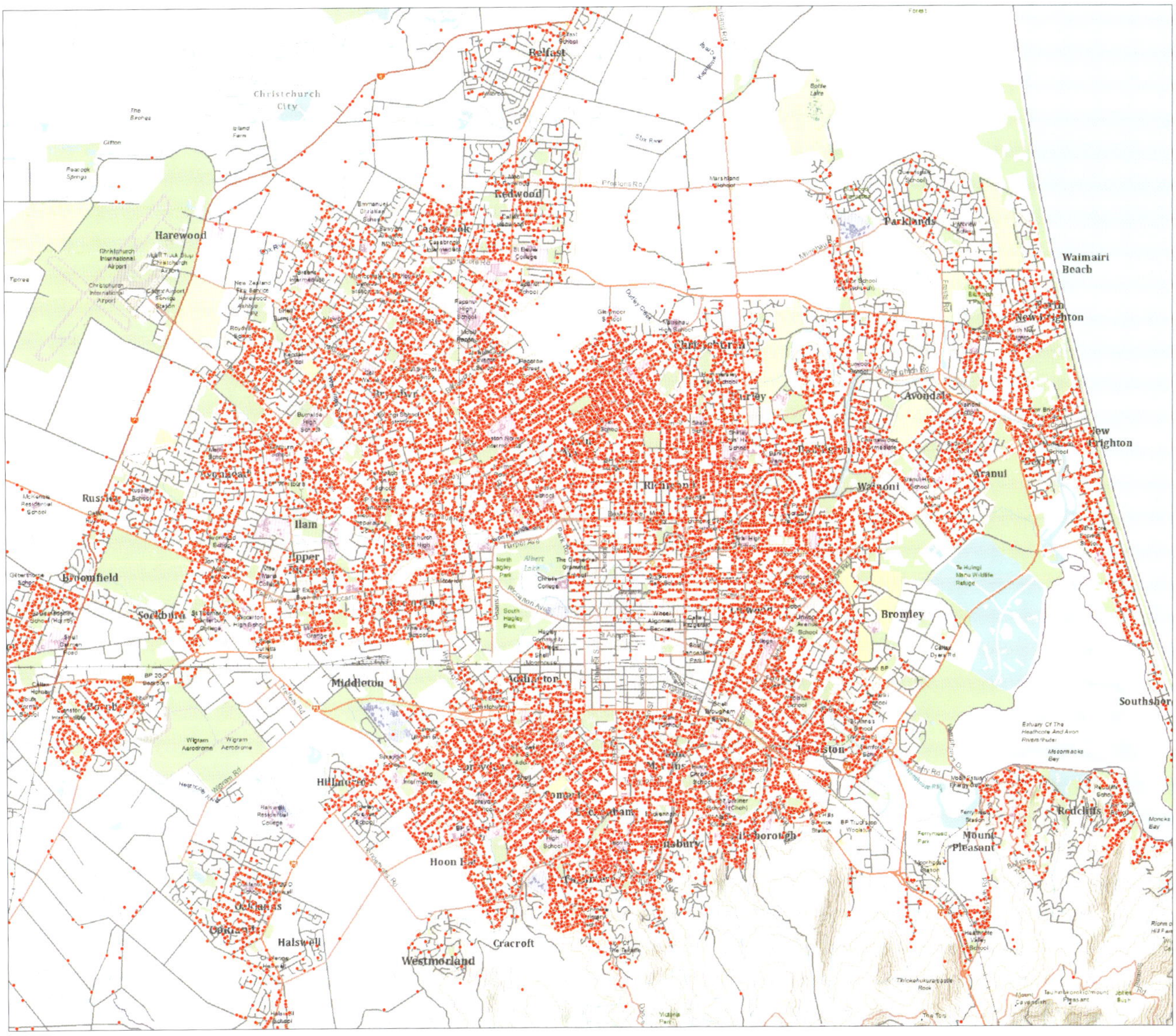

EQC Business Information Unit/Eagle Technology

for householders with home insurance the EQC was obliged to restore an earthquake-damaged property to its previous condition. This example of a rebuilt chimney is in Fisher Avenue, Beckenham.

An even better solution advertised not long after the September quakes involved attaching thin slices from authentic old bricks to a light timber or metal frame. This restored the appearance of the old chimney at only a fraction of its original weight. Heritage Chimney Replacements found a ready market for their solution among owners of historic homes.

Other owners, however, decided not to restore their chimneys and simply had the roof replaced without them. For some significant buildings like Cecil Wood's Bishopscourt (*below*) this would seriously compromise their appearance and heritage value. His Weston House in Park Terrace (*bottom*) was without its main chimney when this photograph was taken. Compare these photographs with those on p.58.

Christchurch celebrated Christmas 2010 with a sense of relief that the aftershocks had been declining in both strength and frequency, and people were looking forward to a New Year free from tremors.

Then came the Boxing Day aftershocks. One of these reached magnitude 4.9 and many people swore that the shaking was more violent than that of 4 September. Others simply swore. Certainly the 10.30am quake on 26 December 2010 was a nasty one. I was in the back garden watering a new lemon tree. The first shake threw me off balance and I had to put my hand against the side of the house to steady myself. Looking up, I saw something I had never seen before. Behind our neighbour's back fence is a stand of mature trees: tall willows, sycamores and silver birches. These were swaying back and forth, like someone waving a bunch of flowers. I could distinctly hear the loud swishing noise they made. Then the tremors stopped and for a few seconds there was total silence. Even the birds were mute, or had fled.

Many brick chimneys that had apparently survived the September earthquakes now showed cracks, while others simply collapsed. My favourite chimney on the corner of Rhodes and Rossall streets (*opposite page, top left*) was still standing, but its curved brick top had collapsed, and was later removed.

As had happened in September, blue plastic and industrial shrink-wrap reappeared to hold damaged chimneys together (*opposite page, centre left*).

The aftershocks of the Boxing Day swarm were clustered in or near the central city. A map published in the *Press* showed seven of them in a line running east–west through Cathedral Square. Though the cathedral itself was declared structurally sound, some older stained-glass windows had broken and cracks had appeared on some cornices. Ornamental crosses were removed just to be on the safe side. Backpackers were evacuated from the former *Lyttelton Times* building, and the *Press* building next door suffered more cracking.

Brickwork fell from yet more old buildings in Manchester Street and the police cordoned off the areas thought to be potentially dangerous. Once again, people exchanged stories of near misses and lucky escapes. The City Mall on Cashel Street remained closed for several days, and individual buildings stayed cordoned off for longer. Boxing Day is usually the busiest trading day of the year for some inner-city retailers, but in 2010 they had to stand by helplessly while engineers checked the damage.

Even after Boxing Day there were some stalwart survivors. Blackheath Place (*below*) in

Sydenham was still looking good, though all its chimneys were now capped and non-functional.

In our street this 10-year-old rebuilt chimney (*below*) still stood proudly, and around the corner this stalk on a Dutch-barn-style residence (*bottom*) appeared to be as solid as ever.

The supports on these chimneys at the St Andrew's College Preparatory School's office had done their job well (*below*) but the chimneys were later taken down.

Despite the flimsy wires, the bracing on these 1960s chimneys in Ilam (*bottom*) seemed to have

saved them.

This three-pot stack was still standing (*left*) but our second chimney had broken at the gather.

By now most of our neighbours had removed the stumps of their broken chimneys and had the roof repaired, but there were still a few others waiting for long-term repairs (*below and above right*).

Some lucky people had already had their chimneys replaced under the EECA scheme and sported shiny new log-burner chimney stacks (*below*).

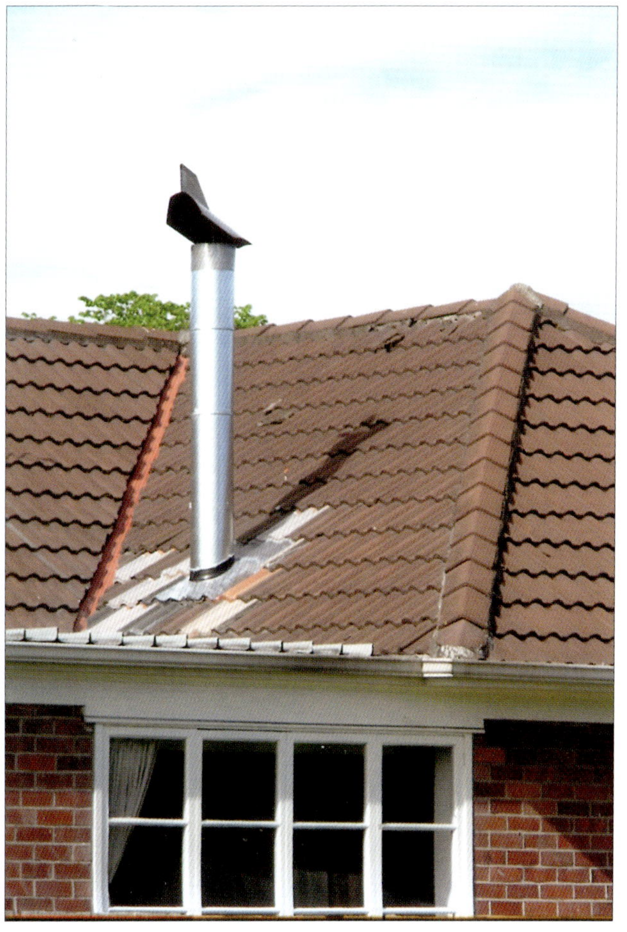

This survivor in Merivale (at left in the photo above) stood alongside the sad remains of what was once a handsome chimney.

In the central city there were some remarkable survivors. At the Arts Centre (*below left and right*), the tall round Oamaru stone chimneys of the old

Registry building of Canterbury University College were still intact, thanks to previous earthquake strengthening, and the two imitation medieval chimneys at the south end of the Great Hall were unscathed, even though a nearby turret had been badly damaged and a crane had gently lowered it to the pavement for repairs.

On Worcester Boulevard, opposite the Arts Centre, these wonderful old chimneys (*above and top left*) had been damaged but were secured to await restoration. Their combination of Homebush pots and terracotta decorative bricks (presumably from the same Glentunnel pottery) was now almost unique in Christchurch.

Around the corner in Gloucester Street (*above right*) these sturdy English square pots with their distinctive spikes had also survived the many aftershocks.

At the end of Park Terrace, these three chimneys on the 1912 McKellar house (*above*) survived because they had steel straps around them. Two heritage chimneys on the former Fleming house (1926) (*following page top*) frame a fine four-chimney stack on the new apartments in Dublin Street.

Out in the suburbs, at the lower end of Linwood Avenue, this 1850s brick mansion known as Linwood House (*above*) was largely hidden from view by the houses that had been built on its former lawns and gardens. Its walls suffered considerable damage, but amazingly its chimneys had survived, together with their Homebush pots, and this unusual nineteenth-century pot, which looked as if it would be more at home on an old steam locomotive than on a house.

Christchurch began 2011 hoping that the earth had gone back to sleep: there were fewer aftershocks during January, and not many were strong enough to be noticed. But the earth's crust had another surprise in store for this shaken but recovering city.

On Tuesday 22 February I was sitting in my third-floor office at the University of Canterbury finishing my lunch with a banana and reading over my notes for a lecture at 1pm when the building began to shake. As the violence increased and I held my computer screen to stop it from falling over I thought, 'This is no aftershock – this is another major earthquake.' No alarms rang, for the power had been cut. A few books tumbled

 ALL FALL DOWN   Christchurch's Lost Chimneys

from a shelf, but most of my shelves were empty. After moving from a large office to a smaller one I had left most of my books in cardboard boxes, stacked on the floor. With retirement looming I saw no point in unpacking. That lazy decision saved me from a shower of books on my head. As the shaking continued I heard shouts and screams from below as students and staff evacuated the building. I could hear colleagues running along our floor, keen to get outside. When the shaking stopped I finished my banana and ventured into the dark corridor. Plaster and roof panels littered the foyer, and as I went downstairs I wondered if the staircase would collapse under me. But it held firm, and I joined my colleagues on the south side of the History building. Several strong aftershocks followed, and a man in a security vest came running past, telling us all to evacuate the campus.

It took me over an hour to drive home, a journey that normally takes 10 minutes, through streets clogged with traffic as anxious parents went to collect their children from school. Text messages had told me that all my nearest and dearest were alive and well, but the car radio brought grim news of collapsed buildings and many deaths in the central city. As I sat in the line of traffic I had plenty of time to inspect the rooftops. For several blocks not a single chimney was left standing, but as I neared home I spotted a few sturdy survivors, mostly on newer houses. All the older brick chimneys had gone. Much to my amazement our dining room chimney was still upright, presumably held together by its reinforcing rods and propped up by the roof timbers. The street was awash with grey silt from liquefaction (*above*).

The next few days were a blur of activity. We

were among the lucky ones who still had power
and water, so our house became an aid-station for
my extended family. My elder sister lives in North
Brighton, where there was no water, power, phone
or sewerage. As an asthmatic she needs to use a
nebuliser machine twice a day, and fortunately
the main roads were clear enough to allow her
son to bring her over to us on the Wednesday. We
invited her to stay, but no, she preferred to sleep
in her own bed. Her house had sunk at one end
and the streets all around her were distorted by
liquefaction. The earth had squeezed the concrete
surrounds of sewerage inspection manholes up to a
foot above the road surface.

We made lunch for 10 people that day, and
helped neighbours to shovel silt from their properties. My elder son generously invited all his school
friends to come and recharge their cellphones, then
surprised us by baking scones to feed them. He
spent the next day making bread, before volunteer-
ing to help at an aid station in New Brighton. My
younger son went off to help with the clean-up
at his school. That weekend we joined the 'Farmy
Army' and exhausted ourselves shovelling silt in St
Albans along with hundreds of other volunteers.
This was an area where I had photographed surviving chimneys after the September earthquake.
Now there were scarcely any left standing.

My daughters live in Linwood, not far from
Stanmore Road, where brick shops had collapsed
and the heritage library building was badly damaged. (One of its chimneys was still standing, but
with a drunken lean [*above right*].)

Fiona's kitchen was a mess, with broken glass,

jams and preserves mingled on the floor, so we
spent an afternoon putting her place to rights. I
still hadn't heard from friends and colleagues living
in the badly affected suburbs of Sumner and Mt
Pleasant, where rock-falls had added to the devastation. I was saddened to see a TV image of Shag
Rock reduced to a small stalk of stone and a heap of
rubble – it was soon being called 'Shag Pile'. Lyttelton had been hard hit, and some of the historic
buildings that had featured in my illustrated history
of the port town were now in ruins, including the
1876 Timeball Station, New Zealand's sole surviving example of this Victorian technological marvel.

As the death toll rose and the number of
those missing remained at well over 200 we all
knew that this had been a far more serious event

than that of September 2010. In retrospect that earthquake now seemed like a gentle rehearsal for the deadlier event.

Not only had many more chimneys come down. In some cases, so had the house. At 277 Papanui Road (*above*) there used to be an elegant two-storey brick house with distinctive double bay windows and splendid big chimneys. The gatepost bore the name 'Larel'.

The February earthquake completely wrecked this fine residence (*above right and below right*). The front chimney had disappeared into the rubble as the house 'pancaked', the upper floors collapsing into the lower. The owner told me his wife had been inside and had narrowly escaped through the back door as the house crashed down behind her.

Within a week the rubble had been taken away and the site scraped clear.

This big house on the corner of Knowles Street and Papanui Road had lost the top of its chimney back in September. Now the entire chimney had come down onto the front lawn, exposing the interior of an upstairs bedroom.

In our own street (*bottom left*), neighbours had been about to take down that unusual three-flue survivor from 2010. The chimney had very obligingly fallen neatly into the builder's skip.

There were no such neat solutions in the central city. Christchurch's CBD had been devastated. While the Red Zone remained cordoned off we could only catch glimpses of the streets from TV news footage, and it was often hard to recognise which thoroughfare was being filmed when only a few familiar buildings remained intact. As the rescue phase sadly gave way to the recovery phase, and all hope of finding anybody still alive faded, news teams were taken by bus to designated points within the Red Zone, and the full extent of the devastation began to unfold.

The first inner city zone to be opened to the public was the west zone, including the Arts Centre. Traffic was confined to a single loop, to enable residents and business owners to recover their possessions. I walked across a deserted Hagley Park and made a tour on foot. The Arts Centre had suffered much more extensive damage this time. The Observatory in the South Quadrangle had collapsed and the Clock Tower would surely have fallen if it had not been braced by massive supports since the Boxing Day/September quake. Surprisingly, the medieval-style chimneys on the Great Hall had survived, but many other tall features had fallen (*opposite page, top and bottom*). On the Old Registry building on the Worcester/Montreal corner two of the Oamaru stone chimneys had crashed down, but the others were still in place.

Nearby, on Montreal Street, this rebuilt

brick chimney (*above*) looked just fine, but most of the others in that block had come down, including those rare terracotta panels on Worcester Boulevard.

At Cranmer Square the former Christchurch Girls' High School building had been encased in scaffolding (*below*), as the September damage had begun to be repaired, but now it looked irreparable.

But for me the saddest sight was on Durham Street, where the Provincial Council Buildings (*opposite page, top*) lay in ruins. Mountfort's marvellous stone debating chamber with its two tall chimneys had imploded, and the red-stone tower on Armagh Street, from which Dr Barker had taken his 1860 panorama of the infant city, had tumbled into the street. Yet the earliest 1850s wooden parts were still standing (*opposite page, bottom*). Surely something could be salvaged and restored on this historic site?

Over the next few weeks, as I ventured across and around the city, revisiting the many houses that appear in this book, I grew numb with sadness at the gaps I found. Nearly all the old brick chimneys had gone, including the very earliest, such as those on Englefield in Fitzgerald Avenue, or Linwood House. The latter had been propped up, but the damage was so deep it finally had to be

demolished. In Bealey Avenue the England house had collapsed, following the fate of its chimneys, and George Gould's three-storey mansion Hambledon had to be demolished. And so the list could go on, but it becomes too depressing to catalogue so many losses. After all, these were merely chimneys, piles of brick and mortar. Nothing could compare with the loss of human lives, and the plight of survivors whose world and livelihoods had been changed forever.

Kiwi ingenuity in Hillsborough.

Survivors, Newcomers and Reminders

This will be a very slim chapter, as so few Christchurch chimneys have survived the February 2011 earthquake. Many of those that adorn Chapter Two no longer exist, and even the two previously well-braced examples in Chapter Four from Normans Road and Ilam have been

taken down. Most vulnerable were the unreinforced Victorian and Edwardian brick chimneys in the city's older suburbs – Addington, Sydenham, Waltham, Linwood, New Brighton, Richmond, St Albans, Merivale, Papanui, Fendalton, Riccarton and Cashmere. In the post-war outer suburbs, especially to the west, such as Hornby, Avonhead, Burnside, Bishopdale, Redwood and Belfast, a surprising number of plain concrete block and stucco chimneys have survived, presumably because reinforcing steel was commonly used in their construction after the 1960s.

Our own dining-room chimney (*above*), declared a hazard by the EQC inspectors back in November 2010, was still there after February 2011, held up by its reinforcing rods and the surrounding roof timbers.

We had asked a builder to take it down, and he advised removing the entire structure to ground level. This would have left us with a hole in the floor. Who would pay for a new floor and some new carpet? We asked EQC and they passed us on to EECA's chimney replacement scheme. They said they would give us a heat pump, but new carpet was regarded as 'betterment' and they wouldn't provide that. Our insurance company said it was earthquake damage and referred us back to EQC. All of these enquiries by email took weeks

to answer, so the chimney was still there to enjoy the February earthquake. By now it had an even more pronounced crack and two bricks had come loose under the roof.

Another EQC inspector in the week following the February quake, a building inspector from Hokitika, was horrified to hear that we still had a brick chimney standing. His memorable advice was, 'Take the bloody thing down, quick and lively, right to the ground!' He had seen over 30 houses with chimneys that had survived the September 2010 shake only to collapse and cause major structural damage in 2011. We contacted the builder again, and he said he had been waiting on the scaffolder, who had lost $200,000 worth of scaffolding in the collapse of various buildings in the inner city, and was having to truck in more from other towns. Our sturdy survivor finally came down in March (*below*), attended by much sweat and dust, as it was

 ALL FALL DOWN | Christchurch's Lost Chimneys

so solidly built that a jack-hammer was needed to break it up. And the EQC finally decided we could claim our damaged carpet under 'contents'.

So the old brick chimneys of Christchurch have indeed become an endangered species, and now that we know we are sitting on an interesting variety of faultlines it would be prudent for home-owners to remove them or have them replaced by lightweight replicas.

Good-looking chimneys continue to appear on new houses, albeit to house the pipe of a log- or pellet-burner, and nearly all of these newcomers came through the 2010 and 2011 earthquakes with flying colours. Here (*above*) is one of my favourites, a very stylish chimney in Papanui.

Also handsome are these metal and timber examples (*top and above*).

Some modern chimneys look like a traditional stack without the row of terracotta pots at the top. Here is one (*above*) with just a single flue, presumably a vent for a gas space heater.

But what exactly is the purpose of these metal frames (*above*) that sit on the top of some new chimneys? An architect has assured me that they have no practical function whatsoever, but became fashionable in the 1990s. He thought they were originally frames for wire-netting to stop birds from falling down log-fire flues, but the look caught on and architects used the framing to extend the height of the chimney for aesthetic reasons.

And then there are the structures that appear to have no practical function but are there to give the impression of a chimney and complete the visual aesthetic of the building (*opposite page*). I have a theory about these fakes or pseudo-chimneys. My guess is that they satisfy a deep psychological need. The shape of a chimney reminds us of hearth and home. Even if there is only a gas heater at the bottom of the flue, or nothing at all, from outside the shape makes us think of a cosy fire, and a cheerful family inside enjoying the warmth.

I heard from a good friend that a new house had been built almost next door to this place in Bryndwr. It was a splendid new house, exactly as the architect had designed it, but when it was finished the owner's wife looked at it and said 'There's something missing. It doesn't look like a *home*. It needs a chimney.' So the builder obligingly, and no doubt at some additional expense, added a structure that resembled a chimney. It has no flue, and no fireplace, but it has a terracotta pot on top, and looks just like the real thing. And the owner's wife was very pleased.

This commercial building (*above*) in Merivale also sports impressive-looking chimneys, which on closer inspection are found to have no practical function at all. But they make the building look suitably traditional in style.

Therefore, rather than deride these structures as fake chimneys, or architects' follies, perhaps we should regard them indulgently as reminders of the chimneys of our ancestors, an echo of the centuries-long tradition of the European chimney.

And what of the future? Is the chimney doomed to disappear from Christchurch streets altogether, destined to become as extinct as the moa? Will Christchurch come to be known as the chimney-less southern capital? Or the flue-free people's republic?

In fact quite a lot of chimneys have survived, especially on the western side of the city, and even a few in the badly affected eastern suburbs. New houses continue to be built with chimney-like structures, whether or not they contain a vent or a flue. There is obviously a future for the chimney in Christchurch. But it almost certainly won't be the familiar brick chimney our grandparents took for granted. It is more likely to look like one of these (*this page top left, above and opposite page*).

Some architects have gone back to the

terracotta pot as a decorative feature on new houses, whether functional or not. These are usually fatter than the traditional New Zealand pot, and one popular style has crenellations. Some look slightly too large for the imitation chimneys they adorn. As far as I know, there are no terracotta chimney pots now being produced in New Zealand. The new ones we see are likely to have been made in Australia, where orange tile roofing and matching terracotta pots are still popular for Federation-style homes. Or they may look like these ones (*below*) from the United States, where the Superior Clay Corporation in Ohio makes both plain and glazed types.

Chimney pots are still being produced in Britain, mainly in the Midlands and North. The catalogue of the National Clayware Federation at one time listed no fewer than 497 different styles of chimney pots, with such intriguing names as Beehive, Cannon Head, Bell Top, Broad-shouldered Roll, Tulip, Fluted Taper, Barrel Top Horned Round Spike, Three Ring Crown Louvre, Hooded Octagonal and Two Piece Bishop.

There is even a chimney pot museum at Cherished Chimneys, run by Lance Bates at Longport, Stoke-on-Trent. He has over 800 collectable pots. The largest collection of English pots was amassed by the Reverend Valentine Fletcher, author of the standard work, *Chimney Pots and Stacks* (1968; paperback, 1994), who initially had 200 pots on display in his garden at Tollard Royal in Wiltshire. His collection grew to over 1000 pots. After his death in 1993 they were moved to the Farm Park Folk Museum at Milton Abbas in Dorset, and were last heard of in the care of the Southampton Brick Museum.

Though the brick chimney may be an endangered species in Christchurch, New Zealand, there is still a future for chimney pots as collectors' items. They look quite small and innocuous when viewed from the ground, but when you break up a fallen chimney you discover that they are quite large and heavy objects, much bigger than an ordinary drainpipe. There is probably little demand for the plain round pots, except as garden planters for herbs or flowers, but the decorated Victorian chimney pot is now surely a candidate for the *Antiques Roadshow*. As some Christchurch homeowners have known for decades, a well-placed antique chimney pot makes an excellent garden feature. Now they will be reminders of the chimney heritage Christchurch lost to the earthquakes of 2010 and 2011.

lte.co.nz
Chim-Lite.co.nz
Replica Chimneys
Chimneys

FURTHER READING

Anderson, J. *A Practical Treatise on Chimneys* (London, 1771)

Beale, D. *Flues and Chimneys* (London, 1973)

Cartwright, P. *Bricklaying* (New York, 2002)

Clavering, R. *Construction and Building of Chimneys* (London, 1779)

Clifton-Taylor, A. *Pattern of English Building* (London, 1972)

Cullingford, B. *British Chimney Sweeps: Five Centuries of Chimney-Sweeping* (Lewes, 2000)

Cullingford, B. *Chimneys and Chimney Sweeps* (London, 2003)

Edwards, F. *A Treatise on Smoky Chimneys, their Cure and Prevention* (London, 1875)

Fletcher, V. *Chimney Pots and Stacks* (Fontwell, 1994)

Franklin, B. *Observations on Smoky Chimneys* (1793)

Hanway, J. *A Sentimental History of Chimney Sweepers* (London, 1785)

Mayhew, H. *London Labour and the Labouring Poor* (London, 1851)

McDonald, R. *The Fireplace Book* (London, 1984)

Osborne, J. *Hampton Court Palace* (London, 1990)

Pickles, W. *Our Grimy Heritage: A Fully Illustrated History of the Factory Chimney in Britain* (1971)

Porter, D. *Considerations on the Present State of Chimney Sweepers* (London, 1792)

Richardson, C. J. *The Englishman's House* (London, 1872)

Salmond, J. *Old New Zealand Houses, 1800–1940* (Auckland, 1986)

Senner, A. H. *Fireplaces and Chimneys* (London, 1941)

Strange, K. H. *The Climbing Boys* (London, 1982)

Traister, J. E. *All About Chimneys: Building, Using, Maintaining and Repairing* (Blue Ridge, 1982)

Williams, G. B. A. *Chimneys in Old Buildings* (London, 1976)

Williams, K. *Stoves, Hearths and Chimneys* (Newton Abbot, 1992)

Wood, M. E. *The English Medieval House* (London, 1981)